MAKE THE MOST
OF YOUR SUN SIGN

Carole Golder

MAKE THE MOST OF YOUR SUN SIGN

For the Librans who helped to bring their balance into my Aries life, the Virgoans who gave me honest and constructive criticism, the Cancerian who sympathised and understood, the Taurean who taught me patience and greater self-discipline, and all my friends in England, Italy and America, from Aries to Pisces, who gave me so much love and encouragement whilst I was writing this book

First published in Great Britain in 1983 by
World's Work Ltd

This edition published in 1988 by
Treasure Press
Michelin House
81 Fulham Road
London SW3 6RB

ISBN 1 85051 290 6

Printed in Austria

CONTENTS

People are often confused because as the Sun doesn't change signs on the same date every year, but can vary between one or two days, the dates given for each sign are approximate. It becomes even more confusing because books, newspapers and magazines often use slightly different dates. If your birthday falls on February 19th and you sometimes find yourself described as Aquarius and sometimes as Pisces, the only sure way to find out if you were born in the last degree of Aquarius or the first degree of Pisces is to have an astrologer check for you by having your exact time and year of birth, together with the place. Astrological charts are calculated using Greenwich Mean Time, which means that time changes between the Hemispheres also have to be taken into account.

ARIES	March 21 – April 20
TAURUS	April 21 – May 21
GEMINI	May 22 – June 22
CANCER	June 23 – July 23
LEO	July 24 – August 23
VIRGO	August 24 – September 23
LIBRA	September 24 – October 23
SCORPIO	October 24 – November 23
SAGITTARIUS	November 24 – December 22
CAPRICORN	December 23 – January 20
AQUARIUS	January 21 – February 18
PISCES	February 19 – March 20

INTRODUCTION

I once met a friend at a cocktail party in New York, who, when asked by another guest if his star was Aquarius, replied, "It used to be, but I changed it to Libra by deed poll at City Hall." When the questioner, who was a lady with very little sense of humour, replied that she wasn't aware that such a thing could be done, my friend answered that it was possible but expensive. Amazingly, she appeared to believe him.

Of course, if you think about the implications of this you will quickly realize that the astrological sign under which you were born, is probably the only thing about you which can never be changed. You can easily alter your hair colour, your nose, or have a new set of teeth implanted. Some people even decide to change their sex. You can take a different name through marriage, by deed poll, or for professional reasons. You may be able to speak a foreign language fluently, to look years younger than your age, and to take pounds off your weight, but the strong astrological influences in your life will always remain rooted within you. It is only by learning about your particular Sun sign that you will become more aware of your strengths and weaknesses and you will be able to make fuller use of your natural abilities and, if you so wish, to develop some of the coveted characteristics which at present you only associate with others. It is for this reason that I decided to write this book.

You probably know that in order to obtain a completely accurate picture of your personality, it is necessary to have a personal horoscope calculated, based on the date, place and time of your birth. You are not one hundred per cent Aries, Taurus or Gemini, because your Ascendant, plus the Moon and other planets, can all influence your personality, depending on how they relate to your particular chart and to the different aspects they make. However, your Sun sign will *still* be your Sun sign.

The term Ascendant relates to the exact moment you were born, and it is the exact degree of the sign rising on the Eastern Horizon at that time, but it is necessary to use astrological calculations to work this out. Whereas the Moon influences your emotions, the Ascendant tends to influence your inner personality, and sometimes your appearance. Something else, which perhaps you don't know, is that certain planetary transits relate to important times in your life, and one of the major influences is when the planet Saturn first returns to the place it occupied in your natal chart, which it does when you are roughly between the ages of twenty nine and thirty. Obviously without looking at a personal horoscope it is only possible to generalize, but the point I want to make in this book is that this "Saturn return" is a highly important part of your life, and will more often than not coincide with your own inner feelings hinting that it is time for some re-organization.

Whatever your sign, whatever your age, I hope this book will help you to deal with emotional, domestic or career problems in a more objective way. If you are a Capricorn wishing to be a Gemini it contains no magic formula to give you a complete character change, but it will help you to modify certain of your characteristics, which should in turn give you greater peace of mind and happiness. It should also help parents to reach a better understanding of their children, thus enabling them to grow up with a more positive outlook on life.

CAROLE GOLDER

THE POSITIVE YOU

... or how to be more so

March 21 – April 20

ARIES

If you were born within the above dates, even if your exact time of birth gave you a Gemini ascendant, you have the Moon in Virgo, Mars in Leo and Jupiter in Aquarius, you are still an Aries, and will remain so, in this lifetime anyway.

However, you do not have to be one of those aggressive, argumentative, impulsive, headstrong people you may have read about, because you can learn how to be more positive in your attitude to life. This doesn't mean that a magic wand will change you overnight, even if you'd prefer it that way, but that your first lesson is going to be – curb your impatience.

If you really want to change your personality, begin by writing "Patience IS a virtue" on a card and displaying it prominently in your home or office. Do it in red, which is eye-catching and supposed to be your favourite colour. Before you start saying that if you change your personality you might become boring and lose half your friends, don't worry, they may welcome a respite from the fireball of energy who calls them at the crack of dawn to chatter on about a new love affair, how unfair the boss has been, or how well the youngest child fared at school the day before!

It might help to make your new motto "think first" before you lose your temper with someone who annoys you, especially if you realize you are being unfair. Are you continually making excuses for not finishing a job, blaming things on everyone and everything else around you, when in reality having started with enthusiasm you have now become bored, or lost your Aries willpower to succeed?

It may be wonderful to be an idealist in today's world, but perhaps this is also the moment to advise you that if you put complete trust in a total stranger just because he or she has a nice smile, you could be asking for trouble.

Stop going on about being the first sign of the Zodiac for no-one is going to dispute it. Perhaps, however, you could sometimes learn to take second, or even third place in your day to day life.

If you are tired of hearing some people say, disapprovingly, "Oh, Aries," when you mention your sign, and if you know you are supposed to be great at rising to challenges, why not decide that the rest of the world is going to see an Arien who has learnt that tact and diplomacy can be just as positive as enthusiasm and vitality? They will help to make you more popular too.

Arien personalities who have made their marks upon the world include Gloria Swanson, Bette Davis, Marlon Brando, Hans Christian Andersen, David Frost, Alec Guinness and Elton John.

April 21 – May 21

TAURUS

You are patient, kind and humorous, but if you really want to get on in this world, perhaps you should also move a little faster. It is almost as if because you are an Earth sign you feel your feet should be planted firmly on the ground each and every minute of the day. Why not look at yourself objectively and see what a great deal you have to offer?

Your practical approach means you are nearly always in demand. You would never let anyone down if something important has to be done, for you are highly dependable, but are you really fulfilled in your life?

If you have gone along the same path for so long that deep down you are feeling just a little discontented, could it be your own fault? Do you tend to find yourself in a rut far too easily, and then have difficulty in extricating yourself, possibly because of the fear of change?

You are sometimes scared of taking risks which could jeopardize your security, when deep down you know you have the ability to succeed at whatever you have set your heart on. I remember a Taurean girl who was a brilliant secretary and had worked for many years in the same firm. One day she was given the opportunity to take over an executive position which seemed to be perfect for her, and yet it took her a while to be convinced that she was capable of handling the job. She had been so used to taking orders from her boss that the idea of being in command frightened her, yet needless to say, once she overcame her fear she made a great success of her new appointment.

Perhaps you should learn to be more adaptable. Your love of creature comforts may contribute to your fear of change. It's almost as if you have said – one life, one routine – and stuck to that theme for ever. No one would suggest that you forget about tomorrow, and change jobs, houses, friends overnight, although if you try harder to be more positive in your outlook, which could sometimes include having a touch more optimism and a little less obstinacy, you will probably feel happier.

Sometimes I have heard people call Taurus a boring sign, but Taurus, you're not boring, you're just hesitant to express your warmth and sensitivity, together with your talents, perhaps because you inwardly fear rejection.

Continue to be cautious by all means, as long as you don't stay earthbound all your life.

Many Taureans are drawn to music, and amongst those

who share your sign are Yehudi Menuhin, Irving Berlin, Bing Crosby and Ella Fitzgerald, whilst other well known Taureans include Catherine the Great, William Shakespeare, and Queen Elizabeth II.

May 22 – June 22

GEMINI

Gemini is the sign of The Twins, and is called a dual sign, which seems to give anyone who might have reason to dislike you an opportunity to accuse you of being two-faced. What is it about you that is both exciting and infuriating, lovable and yet sometimes almost selfish?

The basic problem may be that your restless mind is so occupied searching for variety, that happiness may become elusive.

Every sign in Astrology is ruled by a planet, and the ruler of Gemini is Mercury. Mercury was the winged messenger of the Gods, and Geminians are certainly most competent at putting their messages across. No matter what you have to say, it is expressed so convincingly that other people believe every word even if it is untrue. If a customer in a shop finds him or herself being talked into a new outfit which may look wonderful but is perhaps excessively expensive, it is quite likely that the persuasive sales chat will be delivered by a Gemini.

To be a more positive Gemini, why not devote half an hour each morning sitting still and clearing your mind? Perhaps this sounds incredibly easy, and for some people it might be, but not for a Gemini whose mind is so used to darting off at a tangent that probably the only way for him or her to relax would be to take a course in meditation.

However, let's be optimistic about the whole problem.

Organize your thoughts, and then divide a blank sheet of paper into three columns. In the first jot down all you hope to achieve, in the second your current involvements, and in the third what you are prepared to forego in order to concentrate on your new objectives. You will probably still be left with more than most other people could achieve in two lifetimes, let alone one.

To be a more positive and successful person you must "spring-clean" your life. This doesn't mean that boredom will set in, just that you will have taken an important step in putting your life in order.

What you must always remember is that if you have a special talent, you also have the ability to convince other people of its existence, and if you would just learn to channel all your energy in the right direction, you will surprise some of the people who may have accused you of unreliability and even fickleness in the past.

Other people born under your sign include Queen Victoria, President John F. Kennedy, the Duke of Edinburgh, Henry Kissinger, Marilyn Monroe, Judy Garland, Katie Boyle and Paul McCartney.

June 23 – July 23

CANCER

If you were born between June 23 and July 23, and therefore ruled by the Moon, it will be, very likely, impossible to be bright and outgoing all the time.

You may not be able to help those moods which sometimes turn you from a lovable amusing person into a misery. Perhaps you do blame it on the Moon, for she does influence the tides and therefore as your planetary ruler you may feel it is only natural that she also affects you.

The truth, however, may be that sometimes you secretly

revel in feeling sorry for yourself so that you receive sympathy from other people. In order to become more positive, stop being so incredibly sensitive if someone doesn't give you the attention you feel you deserve. Learn to laugh at yourself a little more. You have a great sense of humour when you want to use it, and it is about time you stopped being quite so self-protective.

If you want to present a more positive personality to the rest of the world, try to become more optimistic about life. Your trouble is that you tend to become too dejected if you take a few knocks, and give yourself an excuse to shrink back into your Cancerian shell to hide away from everyone. Don't you realize though that this kind of behaviour is negative? You will miss out on so much fun and excitement too. Once bitten, twice shy, may be your maxim, but surely you don't have to apply it to every single aspect of your life? Besides, who do you think you are kidding? You're not such a softie underneath. You are often quite tough, and definitely a survivor.

One of your most appealing attributes is your loyalty to family and friends. You are very protective about your own little nest, but if the world is going to see the more positive you, perhaps this is the moment to start clearing some of the dead wood out of your life. You often have a tendency to hang on to things long after you should let them go. Being sentimental is fine, but if every single drawer and cupboard in your home is full of items pertaining to memories of your past, it could mean your mind is also clinging to the past. This certainly doesn't mean you have to forget anything you hold dear, but learn to feel more positive about the future because it too will have memories for you one day.

Never let anyone have a chance to accuse you of being too much like your symbol, the Crab, by clinging to people when they may need to feel free. It is important for you to stand on your own two feet and not scuttle around in someone else's shadow.

However, it's wonderful to know people who don't under-estimate the importance of a happy home life, and you are often prepared to give up a great deal for this. Someone who did just that was the Duke of Windsor. Other Cancerians include Charles Laughton, Ernest Hemingway, Louis Armstrong, Ginger Rogers, Gina Lollobrigida, David Hockney and Ringo Starr.

July 24 – August 23

LEO

To dare to tell you how to be more positive is probably to risk the chance of being kicked. Most of you are convinced you are the rulers of the world, certainly of your own little world, and you thoroughly resent any interference. The lion is supposed to be the king of the animals, and because it is your astrological symbol, you seem to feel that you take precedence over the rest of us.

Your pride is there for all to see, but don't you ever remember hearing that pride comes before a fall? Try to be a little less patronizing and over-powering, especially when you meet someone for the first time. Perhaps some of your extrovert behaviour is an act because you don't want anyone to find the slightest trace of vulnerability in your personality. However, that is ridiculous because everyone tends to be vulnerable somewhere. The bossiest and most domineering Leo girl I knew was happiest when her new boyfriend started to give *her* the orders. It was the first time anyone had ever dared to do that, and it worked. They have been happily married for five years now, so you should realize that being positive doesn't mean you always have to take the limelight.

If you have never had your own personal horoscope worked out, and therefore don't know if you have other influences tempering your Leo character, let's proceed on the assumption that you are a fairly typical Lion with a bright and sunny personality who wants to present an even better image to the rest of the world.

You are usually one of the most generous and warm-hearted signs of the Zodiac. However, if you want more respect, perhaps you should spend more time dealing with your responsibilities and less on your social life. Dare one say you are sometimes too fixed in your opinions? At the risk of another kick, I'm afraid it has to be said. Is there such a thing as being *too* positive? In your case, maybe yes. It is fine to be self-assured and a leader, but you sometimes seem to feel that taking second place is beneath you, and that is where you make your mistake. No one can afford to be right all the time, and no one ever is. Stop being such a dictator, look what happened to Mussolini, who was also a Leo.

In astrology, it is often said that we possess some of the characteristics of our opposite signs, even though they may be hidden far below the surface of our own outward personalities. Your opposite sign is Aquarius, the Water Carrier. You may say that you don't want to be unpredictable and unconventional like some of the Aquarians you know. However, just think of the surprise and admiration on your friends' faces if suddenly you were to stop behaving in such a bossy way.

Admiration is important to you, and you usually manage to obtain it in one way or another. Amongst the personalities born under your sign are Lucille Ball, Count Basie, Mae West, Alfred Hitchcock, Danny La Rue, Jacqueline Kennedy Onassis, Yves Saint Laurent, Mick Jagger, Princess Margaret and Princess Anne.

August 24 – September 23

VIRGO

You need a considerable challenge to make you realize your true potential and present a more positive image. That is because some of you born between August 24 and September 23 seem almost to enjoy putting yourselves (and indeed everyone else around you) down with criticism. What on earth makes you worry about the slightest detail? Haven't you realized that to err is human – as long as you learn something from your mistakes and don't repeat them?

Perhaps your first step should be to reflect upon your past and ask yourself if you really have made so many mistakes, or if you are almost trying to punish yourself for things which have never happened. Who said you should be a martyr?

You have such a great sense of humour, why not learn to use it a little more? Stop being a hypochondriac and be more positive about yourself, especially your health. Thinking about problems all the time can almost create them – at least mentally – and Virgoans are usually exceptionally alert and bright. Like Gemini, you are ruled by the planet Mercury, but you have an advantage, because, unlike some Geminians you can usually train your mind to concentrate. Stop taking on the worries of the world, Virgo, you have only been given one pair of shoulders, and if you cannot do anything constructive about your worries, you are wasting time and energy.

Don't be so unnecessarily hard on yourself. Who wants to live with a paragon of virtue other than perhaps, another Virgo? Remember that if you want to be creative it is sometimes necessary to take a few risks. How can you ever develop your talents if you keep doubting yourself to such an extent that you are frightened to reveal yourself fully to the very people who can help you most?

Perhaps it is a mistake for Virgoans to read that theirs is considered the "sign of service". You've taken it literally, and have forgotten that you are also allowed to enjoy yourself. You may have taken your analytical qualities almost to the point of no return, and have almost forgotten how to relax. You could be so busy summing yourself up, not to mention everyone else, that you overlook some of your wonderfully natural qualities.

Obviously leopards can't change their spots, and you can't change from being a Virgo. But you *can* learn to relax a little more. You can accept an interesting invitation which might mean leaving the office ten minutes early just for once, especially if your boss knows you will make up the time the following day. Why not try to see the brighter side of life just a little more often, instead of being pessimistic?

Perhaps you should memorize these words by Oscar Wilde – "Better to take pleasure in a rose than to put its root under a microscope." Do you think he was visualizing a Virgo when he wrote that?

Before you slip back to under-estimating yourself, you should think of a few of the people born under your sign – Queen Elizabeth I, Maurice Chevalier, Sophia Loren, Greta Garbo and Peter Sellers. It has often been said that Peter Sellers was shy and insecure under the surface, but look how he managed to make so many people laugh with his superb comedy performances, losing himself completely in each role. You don't have to alter too much – just learn to appreciate yourself a little more. Other well known Virgoans include H. G. Wells, Lauren Bacall, Sean Connery and Twiggy.

September 24 – October 23

LIBRA

Your sign has always been thought of as well-balanced because your symbol is "the scales", which is rather like saying that all Geminians must be two-faced, or all Pisceans spend their life going in opposite directions.

However, Librans often seem to need someone else to *give them* a balance, otherwise they tend to drift.

In order to present a more positive face to the world, try once and for all to make some decisions for yourself, without asking your husband, wife, lover, friend or boss for advice. Start with something minor first, in case you are scared of making some terrible mistake. If all goes well, you can soon progress to something more important.

You have probably often read that yours is also the sign of peace and harmony. Do you have a habit of walking away from arguments? Is it perhaps that you cannot be bothered to get involved? Laziness is something else you are accused of. I know some Librans who manage to rush around all over the place, looking after homes, families, jobs and themselves with great energy and enthusiasm, but I can also think of many who prefer to cosset themselves to such a degree that they manage to avoid any real hard work. From now on – no more shirking, you work-shy Librans.

There is definitely one attribute you must not lose and that is your sense of fair play. Even if you do hate to become involved in anything which might upset the harmony you need, you usually try to prevent advantage being taken of anyone else unjustly.

It is really all back to the balancing act, and to making sure that the Libran scales are level. Perhaps this is the moment to tell you that every sign tends to have some of the characteristics of its opposite sign. They may be hidden deep down inside your personality, but they are there. It wouldn't hurt you therefore to sometimes be a little more like one of those noisy energetic Ariens. You may dislike the very idea, but if you could gather up just a little of the Aries vigour and vitality without allowing it to submerge your own personality, it could have the desired effect on someone you have long been trying to impress but who is becoming impatient with your vagueness.

If you read the Aries chapters, you know that "Patience is a Virtue" is a motto particularly applicable to that sign, but what about something like "Procrastination is the root of all evil" as a precept for Librans?

Learn to be more honest with yourself about money. Isn't it time you made a resolution to be slightly less extravagant, and to avoid stopping in front of every shop window which is filled with beautiful things?

Do you realize what being more positive can do to your life? No more wondering if you have made the right move? No more buying a sweater one day and going back the next morning to change it because you are not sure about the colour. No more huge phone bills because you have called up half your friends to ask them if they really think you are making the right choice of partner?

Venus, Goddess of Love, presented you with a wonderful gift – invariably looking good. It is as if the years pass you by with hardly a sign; think how marvellous Brigitte Bardot appears today, whilst Marcello Mastroianni is almost as much of a heart-throb now as he was years ago. Other famous Librans include Sarah Bernhardt, Oscar Wilde, Roger Moore, Julie Andrews, John Lennon and Margaret Thatcher.

October 24 – November 23

SCORPIO

If being positive means being determined – you should not have too much to learn. You certainly know how to protect yourself – could that relate to the symbol of the Scorpion which rules your sign? However, unless you have the Moon and the Ascendant, together with a few other planets also in Scorpio, which would be fairly unlikely, you are going to have your vulnerable points too.

Most people have heard about your famous "sting in the tail" which is a rather unfair description. You are often one of the most loyal signs of the Zodiac. You forgive wrongs to an extent, but if someone really hurts you or someone close to you revenge certainly comes to the fore. There would be little use in asking you to forget a slight, but perhaps you should try just a little harder to turn the other cheek.

You must not be destructive, either to yourself or to anyone else, or be so suspicious to other people, especially when you are in love. Remember that jealousy is an incredibly negative feeling, and points to insecurity. You have to be more positive.

Few people seem to think of a Scorpio as being insecure. You are often described as the sex symbol of the Zodiac, and can certainly be mean, moody and magnificent too. You may be extremely psychic, or at the very least, intuitive. You see deeply into life and sometimes it worries you. You may not like to show your own feelings too much, but you are adept at finding out what is going on in someone else's mind.

As you feel everything so deeply, it would help you sometimes to try and take life a little less seriously. You don't have to audition as a comedian to prove you can make people laugh, but a little less interest in the darker side of life, and

13

a little more in the joys it can bring, could do you a great deal of good. Come on Scorpio, where is your sense of humour?

There is definitely one aspect of your character which is positive — you know what you want from life and will usually go after it without any fear at all. This, however, may lead to recklessness. Did you know that the Scorpion will even sting himself to death when surrounded by a ring of fire? You might not go to those lengths, but it certainly would not do you any harm to become a little more flexible.

Having told Librans to be more decisive, it is time to tell you, Scorpio, to modify your strong will and determination when deep down you know you are taking a wrong path. Admit that you don't like being told what to do, especially as you consider yourself invincible, but remember that most people need a few words of advice at some time in their lives.

Don't be like the Scorpio client who, whilst agreeing profusely with all the problems I had seen in his horoscope, told me he would never make the same mistakes again, and yet appeared a few months later with the same problems. This time they were harder to resolve, because he had gone on and on charting his own course to destruction.

Why not try to soften your personality a fraction? So many things have been written about your brooding resentment and suspicious mind that perhaps people should not be blamed for backing away when you reveal your sign.

Remember, however, that Marie Curie, Charles de Gaulle, Indira Gandhi, Katherine Hepburn, Richard Burton, Luchino Visconti, Nehru, Picasso, Theodore Roosevelt, Vivien Leigh, and Prince Charles were all born between October 24 and November 23. Never forget, either, that your sign has two symbols — first the Scorpion and second the Eagle, which represents your power to rise above the temptations of your lower nature. You can be an Eagle soaring to the heights, or you can be a secretive Scorpion hiding away out of the light. The choice is up to you.

November 24 – December 22

SAGITTARIUS

"Positive, positive! What on earth do you mean? How can anyone be more positive than me?" might easily be a typical reply from a Sagittarian who reads the first few pages of this book.

Perhaps that is the trouble with some of you, you tend to think you know all the answers. It is often true though that Sagittarius is one of the most positive signs in the Zodiac, for you have masses of optimism, an adventurous disposition, a sense of humour, and an almost unfair amount of lucky breaks thanks to the influence of your ruler Jupiter, the planet of good fortune.

However, it is not being positive to insist on moralizing at everyone else simply because they don't see things your way. Why should you set yourself up as an example for the rest of us to follow? Also, if other people don't want to trust to luck to the same extent as you, who are you to say they are wrong?

One of the pleasant aspects of your personality is that you are almost incapable of being dishonest, which should be a positive attribute. However, you can sometimes be extremely tactless at the wrong moment, which is something you should try to overcome. Perhaps you don't even realize what you have said until you notice the mortified look on your listener's face. Honesty is one thing, but telling people the reasons why you feel their lives are disastrous when your opinion hasn't been requested should be avoided.

I once had a client who came to see me feeling terribly upset because her best friend, a Sagittarian, had decided to tell her all the bitchy things her workmates were saying behind her back. It was very obvious from the client's horoscope that she was extremely creative, and equally obvious that there would be times in her life when she would encounter jealousy from other people because of her undeniable success in everything she undertook. In this case, the workmates who were talking about her had probably just learned my client had received promotion and simply had to think of something nasty to say. However, the well-meaning Sagittarian hadn't bothered to think about that, and so it is sometimes necessary for you to be a little more careful before hurting someone unwittingly with some tactless remarks.

One of the marvellous aspects of being a Sagittarian is that you are definitely a survivor. You can suffer setbacks which would send the rest of us reeling and which might take us months to get over. Never lose your wonderful belief in life and all the good things it has to offer you, it is one of your most positive characteristics. Of course, it also helps you to know that you usually manage to look much younger than your real age!

Many Sagittarians gravitate to show business – perhaps it is that lucky streak which enables you to shoot your Sagittarian arrow right to the top. Maria Callas, Frank Sinatra, Noel Coward, Sammy Davis Jnr., Simon Bates, Ronnie Corbett, Jane Fonda and Walt Disney were all born under your sign; but you're also prepared to do your bit for the world in other ways – think of Edith Cavell and Winston Churchill, two more Sagittarian Archers who were determined to make their mark.

If you are a typical Sagittarian, I think it is unlikely that you can honestly say you have never been tactless, inconsiderate, too much of a moralist, or too independent. Being positive doesn't always mean overcoming negative characteristics such as indecision or laziness, and you may sometimes have to overcome other inborn traits.

December 23 – January 20

CAPRICORN

Have you ever felt you were singled out to be one of the real workers of the world? Does life sometimes seem unfair? Would you like to have more fun? The truth is that even if you sometimes think of shirking, your inner soul will not allow it.

You are more than willing to work hard to achieve your ambitions, but don't expect success to be presented to you on a golden platter, even a silver one, unless you deserve it. However, is it really necessary to shut yourself off from the lighter side of life, and creep into a shell as if you were your opposite sign of Cancer? There may not be very much to smile over when you read the newspapers or watch television, but if you continually see the world in a gloomy light it is bound to affect your own personality.

Perhaps you are feeling insulted that your behaviour should be criticized when you are only trying to do your best for all the people closest to you; that as far as you are concerned a sense of responsibility is important; and that you are not being narrow-minded but sensible. I would like to point out that if you stop being such a pessimist you can enjoy your life *and* work hard as well. Pessimism is negative, and the whole point of this book is to try and help you make the most of your Sun sign.

Your ruling planet is Saturn, who in ancient mythology was Saturnus, god of agriculture and founder of civilization and social order for the Romans, and who was identified with Cronus, the Greek God of Time and of mundane time cycles. Saturn is depicted as the reaper, the time-keeper, holding the hour-glass and the scythe, and astrologers often tend to think of him as Father Time. Time *is* of great importance to you, although not in the way that Ariens and Geminians necessarily think of it. It doesn't mean rushing about all over the place, but it does involve planning every-thing you do extremely carefully. You don't usually mind how long it takes you to achieve your objectives as long as they are achieved, and with Saturn's influence you tend to reap the benefits of your labours in the end.

However, the influence of Saturn doesn't have to seem like a supervisor who makes you clock in at a certain time, and refuses to allow you to clock out a minute too early. Have you never considered that a short break could enable you to get on much better with your tasks later?

Your sense of duty is a great attribute, but don't think of yourself as a martyr, and look on askance when other people are enjoying themselves! Dr. Martin Luther King and President Anwar Sadat were certainly two Capricorns who tried to achieve peace in recent years. Others who have made names for themselves in other areas include Muhammed Ali, Marlene Dietrich, Nat 'King' Cole, Anton Rogers, Helena Rubenstein, Ethel Merman and Federico Fellini.

January 21 – February 18

AQUARIUS

Aquarians have been defined as people who are wonderful when you expect them to be difficult and the contrary when you felt everything should run smoothly. Perhaps this is being unfair, but the fact that you are one of the most unconventional and unpredictable signs of the Zodiac is certainly true. If being positive means originality in thought and independence in manner, you have a great deal to offer.

Don't you think, however, you should make more of an effort to conform with the rest of the world? It is all very well to be an idealist and a rebel with a cause, but sometimes your ideas can be too futuristic and you waste time on impracticalities.

You really do care about the suffering masses in the world, and should be proud to be known as the "humanitarian" of the Zodiac. I wonder, though, whether you give enough attention to your immediate family or your dearest friends? Your rather detached manner creates the wrong impression. You certainly have a warm heart but sometimes have difficulty revealing your innermost feelings. You always believe firmly in truth, fair deals, and equality which is very positive.

Your planetary ruler is Uranus, who was the God of the Heavens, personified as the "sky at night" by the Greeks in their mythology. The planet itself was discovered in 1781 by Sir William Herschel, and its symbol relates to the H of his surname. The discovery of this planet coincided with new scientific discoveries and inventions, and Uranus always is associated with change, independence and invention. However, it is also said that Saturn has an influence on your sign, acting as a restricting force which is needed to calm down the more rebellious tendencies of some Aquarians.

Three American presidents, Abraham Lincoln, Franklin Roosevelt and Ronald Reagan, were born under your sign, whilst other famous Aquarians include Thomas Edison, Charles Lindbergh, Jules Verne, Somerset Maugham, Zsa Zsa Gabor, Vanessa Redgrave, Yoko Ono, and Bill Gibb.

The world needs more outward looking people. Why can't you manage to combine the idealistic and inventive characteristics of your personality with a little more realism, and try even harder to show tenderness and understanding to the people with whom you share your personal life.

Being positive doesn't consist solely of taking a firm stand on the issues you believe in, it often means you should be more prepared to see both sides of a situation, and have a more balanced approach to life.

February 19 – March 20

PISCES

It is time to learn that just because you consider yourself a gentle Water sign ruled by the inspirational planet Neptune, it is neither necessary nor wise for you to drift through life as if you were floating in the sea, taken wherever the tides might choose.

"Yes, I know I'm impractical, I just can't help it," you say, when yet again you have to borrow some money from your long suffering friends.

You are quite content to go on in this way, being kind and sympathetic to people less fortunate than yourself, and it is heartening to find a true romantic in a world which seems to have lost so much of its own romance.

You don't, however, have to turn into a bossy Leo or a moody Cancerian. You can be emotional and creative without being careless, and isn't it better to be financially secure than always to be worrying about the housekeeping bills?

First of all, take off those rose-coloured spectacles, those which astrologers through the ages always accused you of wearing. They create an illusion, and perhaps life looks better so, but you can't afford illusions any more. Try to sift the practical from the impractical, you will be surprised how much easier it will make your life.

You often possess talents, which for one reason or another you prefer not to develop. Perhaps it's a fear of rejection, so why not be a little more like an Aries and try to thrive on challenges? Because you are number twelve in the Zodiac it doesn't mean you have to come in last when they are handing out prizes for success.

Try not to be quite so receptive to other people's influences, unless you are absolutely certain they are for your own good. Sometimes you forget that you possess an intuition bordering on the psychic, and being able to sum up people extremely well is a great advantage when used properly.

I remember reading something once by Oliver Wendell Holmes which applied to Pisces — "A moment's insight is sometimes worth a life's experience." However, Pisces, it is necessary to make use of that insight, don't just file it away in your scrapbook full of dreams. Besides, no one is telling you to *stop* being a dreamer, only to try and turn your fairy tales into reality, if you can.

It's not necessary to stop being a romantic even if you could. Think of Michelangelo, Renoir, Elizabeth Barrett Browning and Chopin — all romantics in their own specific ways. Elizabeth Taylor, Rudolf Nureyev, Marcia Falkender, Ronald Searle, Lord Snowdon and Liza Minelli have also turned their Piscean talents into successful careers.

CHILDREN OF THE ZODIAC

... the first years

Perhaps you feel your own life could have been made easier if only your parents had known something about Astrology? They would have realized that your childhood shyness might have stemmed from being born under the sign of Cancer, or that your constant showing off only meant you were a Leo anxious for attention.

I believe that every child shows some of his or her Sun sign characteristics from a very early age, and knowing more about your infant's astrological influences should help you to understand the talents and tendencies that he or she may show.

From headstrong Aries to dreamy Pisces, we are all rather like pebbles on a beach, for the likelihood of finding two people exactly the same is very small indeed. Even twins are not born at exactly the same time, which means that their Ascendants could be different, and there may be slightly different planetary aspects, if in that fraction of time, the Moon or another fast moving planet had entered another sign.

The way we behave later in life is almost always influenced to some extent by our childhood. Perhaps it is easy to blame our parents for certain things, but knowing more about astrology should also be of help. It doesn't mean you have to rush straight out for a precise horoscope for your child, drawn up by a professional astrologer. Always remember that even with astrology there is also free will. It is all very well to see from a child's birthchart that he or she shows musical talent, but perhaps that child is only seven years

old and doesn't want to sit in front of a piano for two hours a day. Encourage, but don't push.

If you are interested in having birthcharts done for your children, try to use them as guide lines, certainly until the children are of the age to at least participate in making decisions, and a guide line can certainly be helpful.

It is never too early to be guided in the right direction, and perhaps all our lives could have been spared a few crises if our own sun sign characteristics had been recognized when we were children too.

The first years
ARIES

Lots of children cry, but what is it about an Aries baby whose first breath is so often followed by a yell that starts the nurses running to and fro? It's almost as if an Aries child expects the red carpet to be laid down instantly, and would like a roomful of servants to cater to his or her every whim. Don't despair, however, for a scream can just as easily turn into a beaming smile when the attention your child so obviously desires is forthcoming.

You probably already know enough about astrology to have learnt that Aries is the first sign of the Zodiac, co-inciding with the first day of Spring, and that Ariens are thought of as leaders, which perhaps is a reason for your newborn infant to insist on making his or her presence known from the start. Aries is a Cardinal Positive Fire sign, which basically means Ariens are energetic, assertive, enter-prising and self-expressive. Never forget, though, that even if these children seem to be born saying "me first", they are unlikely to be as self-confident as they may appear. They can also be unsure of themselves, and a forceful personality may be trying to hide a plea for love and attention.

Ariens need loving but firm hands to guide them on their way through life, but perhaps it would also help you to understand your child better if you realize that the ruling planet of Aries is Mars, who was the God of War in mythology. It is almost as if the influence of Mars makes it appear that an Arien likes nothing better than a battle.

However Aries children must learn that the planet Earth isn't necessarily a battle field. There will be time when they grow up to read about the atrocities of war, or to see them on television screens. They need to know that they belong in a family and home which will shelter them, whilst preparing them for some of the knocks they may have to face later on.

It is important, therefore, for your Aries child to feel secure. Even the smallest babies may need discipline, but make sure you hand it out together with a great deal of love and affection. As the months turn into years, try not to force your child into something against his or her will without giving a good explanation, and always endeavour to give praise when deserved.

Everyone can be accident prone, but from an early age you may realize you have given birth to perhaps one of the most accident prone signs, often because Ariens are always in such a hurry. Astrologically, Aries rules the head, and all those words like headstrong, headlong, head first, seem to have been invented just for Aries, so don't be surprised if your child seems to be especially prone to bumps and bruises in addition to the usual childhood illnesses.

Try not to be one of those parents who insist on baby talk with your Aries infant, for it is unlikely to be appreciated. If you insist on playing it your way, you only have yourself to blame if a mouthful of food lands on your lap, or a yell of annoyance pierces your ear drum.

There is one thing you should never forget, an Aries child needs to have some make-believe in his or her life, being idealistic as well as headstrong. Fairy tales and Father Christmas, Alice in Wonderland and the Wizard of Oz,

knights riding up on white horses to rescue princesses, all belong in the world of Aries children.

The first years

TAURUS

If you are the parent of a Taurus child, you probably discovered that he or she came into the world with a very determined mind.

However, with Venus, Goddess of Love, as the planetary ruler of this sign, your child will also have a sweet and loving side. The first smile will often be worth a photograph, and you will usually have no reason to complain about a lack of affection.

Taurus is a Negative Fixed Earth sign, which basically means Taureans tend to be practical, steadfast, self-restrained and passive.

Taurean children are often a joy to be with because they can be so placid and sweet natured, and adore to be hugged and cuddled. You may not have to spend too many sleepless nights, although if it is time for a nappy change and baby Taurus doesn't feel like being disturbed, that's when the stubborn side of the Taurus personality may emerge. All children need to understand that there is a reason for everything, so Taureans too will respond to your wishes much more willingly if they know "why".

A happy home atmosphere is important to everyone. Taureans are very sensitive, even though they may not necessarily appear so on the surface, and they want everyone to feel love and to enjoy being together.

As security is important to Taureans, they should obviously learn about it in their own homes. Remember that a Taurus baby needs peace and harmony. Don't let this child

grow up being too possessive about loved ones, and never take favourite toys away without a good reason unless you want to see a real tantrum, although you should teach the importance of sharing with other children.

Taureans tend to develop colour sense early in life, so don't paint your child's bedroom or make him or her wear clothes in colours which he or she dislikes. If you have a garden you will probably discover your Taurean child, like many children, loves to play in it. As many Taureans seem to have been born with green fingers, it is a good idea to give them a special little patch of garden to tend.

Taurus is astrologically related to the throat and neck, and childhood illnesses could include sore throats, tonsillitis and ear-ache and perhaps also mumps.

You may be pleasantly surprised to find your child shows a talent for music or singing. Let him or her have lessons whilst young if possible as the results could be worthwhile, but don't insist if it becomes obvious that your particular youngster is definitely not interested or gifted. This talent usually comes to the surface of its own accord if it is there.

If you give Taurus children all the love, encouragement and rationality they desire, you won't often have to cope with tantrums when you are trying to coax them to do something they hate.

Most of the time your child will probably be well-behaved and a pleasure to bring up. Parents who understand the Taurean need for explanations will certainly help to prevent their children from being labelled obstinate, self-indulgent and stubborn once they grow up.

The first years

GEMINI

Patience is one of the most important requisites for the parents of a Gemini child, followed closely by the realization that you may either have to take a refresher course in the subjects you learned at school, or invest in a good dictionary and a set of encyclopaedias!

Gemini, the sign of The Twins, is a Positive Mutable Air Sign. Interpreting mutable to mean "the tendency to undergo change" it would seem as if the Gemini baby acquires, on taking its first breath of air, a desire for change and variety which will probably last a lifetime.

Whereas Ariens like to be leaders, and Taureans are often happy to follow in second place, as the third sign of the Zodiac, Gemini is primarily concerned with communication. Your Gemini child may not only start asking you challenging questions from an early age, but may start walking almost as soon as crawling, whilst reading, writing and drawing will be unlikely to daunt him or her.

Gemini babies are often wonderfully adaptable to circumstances, tending not to mind being stared at, cooed at, picked up and hugged by admiring visitors. This is because they are equally inquisitive themselves. There is a whole world waiting outside their cribs, and they intend to understand as much of it as they possibly can.

Your Gemini child may appear to be full of nervous energy, and as a parent, it is going to be up to you to harness this energy in the best possible way. Many Geminians grow up to be night people, hating the idea of wasting time sleeping. However, in order to be healthy it is obviously necessary to rest and relax enough, so only by educating your child whilst very young will this objective be achieved. Because Gemini children can be highly strung, try not to have arguments with your partner if you think you can be overheard.

No matter how inquisitive these children are, it would really upset them to think their parents were not getting along.

The nervous and respiratory system is ruled by Gemini, and bronchitis, asthma, pleurisy and pneumonia can be some of the Gemini illnesses. Fresh air is healthy, but watch out that childhood colds and coughs don't turn into anything serious. Always try to get your child into the habit of a regular sleep time, even if it means having to read a bedtime story when you'd rather be watching your favourite series on the television.

In the preface to this book, I said that the one thing it is impossible to change is your star sign. Don't ever start to wish that your Gemini bundle of energy and curiosity would turn into a quieter and perhaps more placid Taurean, or a shy little Piscean. As your baby grows older, together you will see the world in a new light, which will probably even have a rejuvenating effect on you.

Gemini children tend to have an incredible amount of imagination, and have even been known to invent invisible playmates to ensure they won't be lonely. I remember one little boy who was heard by his parents talking to someone whilst he was bathing himself one night. Needless to say there was nobody else in the bathroom, and the strangest part about that conversation was that when asked who he was talking to, he described an Uncle Jim who had died before he was born. His particularly vivid imagination had also combined itself with a psychic quality too.

Never stifle the Gemini imagination, it needs to flourish, but a lot of patience is required to make it flourish in the right direction. Baby Gemini needs to learn that toys taken out and strewn throughout different rooms must be put away, that asking questions is positive only if the answers are listened to as well, and that punctuality is important.

If you combine your discipline with a sense of humour, you won't have too many battles trying to lead your Gemini child along the right path, and you will also have a great deal of fun at the same time.

The first years

CANCER

If you always dreamt of having a child who was sensitive, emotional, loving and imaginative, then you can count yourself lucky to have a Cancerian in your family.

However, it is important to remember that Cancerians sometimes change moods so quickly you may wonder what has hit you. Because of their sensitivity, they need to feel loved, and if misunderstood, even when very small, they will soon retreat into their shells.

Cancer is a Water sign, and is Cardinal and Negative, which basically means that for all the emotional and sometimes self-repressing qualities Cancerians possess, there is also an enterprising side to them. If you are the parent of a Cancerian baby, never under-estimate his or her inner strength. The eyes may fill with tears at the sound of a raised voice, or when it's time for an undesired nappy change, but there is also a stubborn quality.

There are twelve houses in the Zodiac, each relating to a different sphere of life. Cancer is associated with the fourth house, which in turn relates to the home and family. If you have a daughter you should be able to look forward to an extra pair of helping hands around the house, and male Cancerians often become very domesticated.

A Cancerian child may like to be cossetted a little, but don't over-do this or he or she could grow up as someone who sulks and becomes moody if things go wrong. Be tender, and show lots of approval, but be firm too. Let your child know you are there in the background, but that it is also important to learn the meaning of independence.

A secure family background is important, but even if you and your partner were to split up, this need not create problems as long as you both try to give your child the necessary love and attention. If a Cancerian child does come from a broken home, try to ensure that he or she ends up with two homes in which to feel happy. Never let your child feel unwanted. Childhood memories usually stay firmly in the mind for ever, which means that hurts and rejections can stay there too. To be an integral part of a loving family is something most people want, but for a Cancerian child to lack this can be likened to a plant which is not given enough water starting to wither.

Your child's appreciation of everything you do will probably so far outweigh any difficulties you may encounter that on many occasions you could consider yourself blessed. However, it isn't just a joke when people talk about Cancerians crawling into their shells, and you may have to be gentle with your child once it is time to leave the cozy world of home and start to mix with other people. Once your child realizes that meeting other children and learning to share toys and new experiences can be a great deal of fun, you may not have to worry too much about shyness.

Your Cancerian child may be quite a bright little personality on the surface but there is nearly always a dream world for this highly imaginative and intuitive sign. However, the Cancerian imagination can sometimes lead to inner doubts and fears which other people may not notice and this is where your love and understanding are so important. A bedtime story and the knowledge that home is a secure and happy place is the best reassurance for this. Try never to leave your child alone at night in an empty house, even if only for a short time, because waking up frightened could leave a lasting memory.

Healthwise, your child should learn early on the importance of eating properly, because Cancerians are often prone to tummy troubles. Digestive and gastric troubles can plague those who don't look after their health, and, as a parent, you should start the training early.

Remember that even the toughest little Cancerian will probably have a soft heart underneath. Look after your child tenderly but help him or her to develop the sense of humour which is often part of a Cancerian personality because it could be enormously useful in lessening any desire to creep into that mythical shell. Besides, being positive should surely also mean the ability to be able to laugh at oneself, and what better time to learn this than in childhood?

The first years

LEO

Did your baby's first cry sound like a roar to you? Did you have an uncomfortable feeling you should have asked someone to bring a miniature crown for your infant as well as a bunch of grapes for you?

The symbol of Leo is a lion's mane, and Leo is a Positive Fixed Fire sign, which implies that Leos are assertive, spontaneous, self-expressive and energetic. The ruling planet of Leo is the Sun, and whilst you will soon discover that your child's personality can be sunny, lovable and playful, he or she will probably never put up with being ignored.

Everything may depend on how you decide to do the bringing up as, of course, you are in charge, and you should show that you won't put up with any nonsense and give in to unnecessary tantrums so that your little Leo will soon realize you are not at his or her beck and call.

A Leo needs to be taught early on that the world can be a marvellous place, but it hasn't been created just for Leos, there are eleven other signs in the Zoo of the Zodiac, and the Lion must not demand more than its fair share.

Don't worry, you haven't given birth to a bossy little child who is going to upset everyone else at home. Leos don't usually mean to upset anyone with their behaviour, and with a Leo child you certainly shouldn't have many dull moments to complain about.

Besides, that "I'm in charge" image may seem to be very powerful, but underneath it all your little Leo has a heart of gold and a vulnerable nature. His or her personality may sparkle most of the time, but if your Leo child feels unloved or left out in the cold, you will certainly notice the change. It may not be that tears suddenly start to fall, but it could almost seem as if all the light has gone out of your little Leo's face. You have given birth to an emotional child, and should remember this. Your child needs to feel secure and know that you are proud to be his or her parent. Pride is a word which is definitely part of the Leo vocabulary. Leos need to be proud of themselves and also of the people they love.

If you have a Leo daughter, she could be a tomboy, not wanting to be left out of the games the boys play. You may have to watch out that she doesn't start becoming too bossy once she *is* old enough to mix with other children so that she doesn't grow up into one of those domineering women who end up making life miserable for themselves and their husbands.

Perhaps it will also help you to understand your Leo child a little more by realizing there could be something of a conflict in the Leo personality, the enterprising Fire sign sometimes feeling held back by its Fixed quality. The over-domineering side should be played down, whilst the over-generous qualities also need to be tempered slightly once your child is older, especially where they relate to money.

Once your child learns that to be the centre of attention once in a while is fine, but that it won't always happen, you will have fewer problems. You shouldn't try to cramp your child's style, or criticize him or her in front of other children because that can leave a lasting hurt.

A Leo child will often have high spirits and sometimes wear you out with all his or her exuberance and vitality. Healthwise, Leo rules the heart and also the dorsal region of the spine. Leos can be healthy most of their lives, but childhood illnesses may sometimes be accompanied by high

temperatures, and your child should certainly be taught the importance of rest.

If your own childhood didn't contain a great deal of affection, you should soon be delighted you have brought a Leo into the world, for affection is one thing you should never be short of from your child.

The first years

VIRGO

It would be no great surprise to me if Virgo babies entered the world carrying a miniature microscope with which to peer at their parents, for Virgo is *the* critic of the Zodiac.

However, don't misunderstand me, for a Virgo child can be an absolute delight, and once you learn to understand each other, there may not be many of the tantrums or stubborn moods sometimes associated with other signs.

The symbol of Virgo is The Virgin, and is the only feminine figure in the Zodiac. In ancient times Virgo was worshipped as the Earth Goddess, and depicted holding an ear of wheat, the symbol of fertility. She is a Negative Mutable Earth sign, which in layman's terms basically means Virgoans are fairly passive but can be practical and adaptable.

Virgo's planetary ruler is Mercury, who also rules Gemini. However, whereas Geminians can be disorganized in thoughts and ideas, Virgoans are usually much better at training their minds on specific subjects, and it shouldn't be long before you realize that your Virgo child is bright and imaginative.

Perhaps this should also be the moment to advise you that some Virgoans are insecure, and it would be hard for a child to accept that he or she is second best in any way, so if you do have other children, always ensure that little

Virgo is not left out. This doesn't mean a Virgo child expects to be spoilt, but to be treated unfairly or severely scolded for minor reasons will obviously hurt.

Some infants can be fussy at feeding times, but try to be patient and convince your child that even if greens don't taste particularly good when compared with lollipops, it is important to eat the right foods. Once you are believed, it should be smoother sailing. Some Virgoans grow up to be health or food freaks, and although you don't necessarily want your child to do so, you will probably be happy to have someone around who appreciates the value of good nutrition.

The influence of the planet Mercury can often help your child to speak at an early age, for don't forget that Mercury is the planet of communication. However, you must be prepared to answer lots of questions!

A Virgo child may have a big heart, but although a talent for communication means he or she is unlikely to be short of words very often, it is sometimes difficult for a Virgoan to show love with great displays of physical affection. It may be demonstrated in a quieter, less emotional way. Your child may also be somewhat shy, especially when meeting other people for the first time, so don't be too pushy when making introductions, or criticize your little Virgo in front of strangers, for this child is often more sensitive than the other Earth signs of Taurus and Capricorn.

Virgo is the sixth house in the Zodiac, which relates to service, work and health. From an early age your child may be more than willing to help around the house. However, some Virgoans may easily grow up to be hypochondriacs. Astrologically, Virgo rules the abdominal region, the spleen, the intestines and the central nervous system. Your child might also suffer from appendicitis, although obviously not every Virgoan will have this problem. Always try to convince your child that worry is a negative quality and can even cause ill health. Adult Virgoans may even be prone to ulcers through worrying too much. Don't create a drama

every time your child falls over, or catches a normal childhood illness. Obviously, when a child is ill, it is important
to seek advice, but don't rush your little Virgoan along to
the doctor at the very first runny nose unless you feel it
is necessary.

Your Virgo child may love to have a pet, and you certainly
shouldn't have to worry about who is going to look after
it, for Virgoans of all ages tend to be sticklers for
responsibility.

However, if you really want to help your child grow
up into a bright and sparkling adult, make sure your home
is a happy and relaxing place, with plenty of laughter, for
Virgo can sometimes be too serious, and childhood should
be fun even for "the sign of service".

The first years

LIBRA

It sometimes seems as if Librans are born with the ability
to charm everyone in sight. When you first gaze upon that
little face it seems to be smiling sweetly at you, and you
may be convinced that you are going to have the easiest
time imaginable in bringing up your new son or daughter.

I would certainly hate you to be disappointed, but perhaps
a little explanation regarding the qualities of Libra would
be useful at this point.

Ruled by Venus, Goddess of Love, Libra is classified as
a Cardinal Air and Positive sign, which basically means that
Librans should be self-expressive, communicative, mentally
active and fairly spontaneous and enterprising. However,
when you remember that Libra's astrological symbol is the
scales, but that when scales are not balanced properly one
end is higher than the other, you can perhaps begin to understand the personality of Libra more easily.

It will not be long before you realize that your newborn child could turn into an unnecessarily indecisive adult unless you try to help the balancing act from the start. Too many choices are difficult for Libra, and this can even mean deciding whether a teddy bear or rag doll should take pride of place in the cot.

I had a client who was worried that her infant daughter was becoming stubborn, obstinate and lazy because the child seemed to take forever getting dressed once she was old enough to do so herself. The mother had failed to understand that the choice of deciding what to wear was proving a great problem for her daughter. The child desperately wanted to please her mother and to look perfect, but a Libran child may not always be able to make decisions, without being carefully guided in the right directions from the very start. You are fortunate to have a child who may sometimes be one of the most good natured in the entire Zodiac, and stubbornness is not usually a Libran characteristic.

Libra is the seventh house of the Zodiac, and relates to marriage and partnerships. You will soon realize that your child although not necessarily extrovert, won't like to be left alone for too long. Librans love company as long as it is pleasant. The desire for peace and harmony at all costs will be very apparent even whilst your child is still a toddler. Raised voices will be upsetting so try not to have arguments within earshot of your child's room.

A Libran child doesn't expect to be spoilt, but will certainly react if he or she is the recipient of unfair treatment, or sees anyone else being badly treated.

Librans are often accused of being lazy, but it is unfair to classify them all under one heading. You will soon discover, however, that your Libran child hates anyone to say "Hurry up!" Librans like to take their time over everything, and unless you are careful you may find that the sun that was shining beautifully when you first suggested your child should play in the garden, could have disappeared behind the clouds by the time he is ready to go outside. A Libran

should not be pushed into being overly energetic, because to retain the right balance in the physical make up of this sign, it is especially important to have time to relax.

Healthwise, the areas of the body ruled by Libra are the kidneys and the lumbar region. Your child will probably have his or her share of the usual childhood ailments, but with proper attention and a happy peaceful atmosphere recovery should be straightforward. Try to guide your child in the right direction over food for a 'sweet tooth' can be a Libran characteristic, and perhaps lead to natural curves turning to fat in later years.

It won't be long before you discover that your child has an eye for beauty, bestowed on Librans by Venus, who was also identified with Aphrodite, the Greek Goddess of love and beauty. Libran children may be happiest in bedrooms decorated in soft pastel colours away from the loud noise of traffic when this is possible.

A Libran is usually a very affectionate and loving child, provided everyone in the family is treated equally. The Libran sense of fair play also means this child will usually stick up for the under-dog, and it may not be long before your home is filled with stray pets or even other children who are perhaps having a rough time.

Try to be patient once the time does come for your child to make any choices and decisions, even if they seem relatively minor, for your guidance can help to make growing up a great deal easier.

The first years

SCORPIO

The first impression you will have upon gazing at your Scorpion child is one of strength. I am certainly not inferring that your newborn baby is built like a miniature prize fighter, but rather that you will sense an inner strength which radiates from the tiniest Scorpio baby.

Having given birth to your son or daughter, you will have found yourself with a real little individual; and perhaps in addition to "Dr. Spock" and all those other child rearing books which have come in useful to so many parents, you should resolve to learn a lot more about what makes a Scorpio tick.

Other than its astrological symbols, Scorpio is also associated with two planets – Mars, the God of War, and Pluto, the God of the Underworld. It is a Fixed Water and Negative sign, which basically means that Scorpios can be self-repressive, passive, intuitive and emotional, and that their personalities may be both steadfast and intense. The mystery of life and death is often the very essence of being to a Scorpio, and you may soon discover that there is so much emotional energy inside your child's little body that unless it is harnessed constructively in the very beginning, adapting to life could be difficult. This is basically because of Scorpio's desire to uncover the deepest mysteries of life in order to identify more with its source.

By now you may have begun to despair of having an easy time bringing up your child, but providing you are in command, and ensure that discipline is accompanied by love and understanding, you will be well on the way to achieving the right kind of relationship with your child.

Scorpio children can be emotional and temperamental, and there may be tantrums when they don't get their own way, so make sure that you establish a pattern of mutual respect from the start, and never let your little Scorpio feel he or she is "put up with" rather than loved and wanted, as this can lead to bitter resentment in later years.

A Scorpio child is highly intuitive and will always know if something is wrong by just looking at your face or listening to the sound of your voice. You will nonetheless soon discover that if a Scorpio wants to be secretive, there is no way that anyone will find out what is going on behind that impassive face.

Your child will be immensely loyal to you, although if accused unjustly you may discover it takes a long while to be forgiven by a Scorpio even a very young one, and you could be reminded of your mistake even twenty years later.

Scorpio children tend to have masses of physical energy, which should be used positively and not bottled up. Childhood illnesses pass quickly, and it is unlikely your little Scorpio will make much of a fuss over bumps and bruises or even a bleeding nose. The parts of the body ruled by Scorpio are the genitals, bladder, urethra and rectum, which naturally doesn't mean that everyone born under Scorpio is going to have problems there. It is simply that they can be weak areas.

You will soon learn that your Scorpio child has a great deal of intelligence and is anxious to learn as much as possible about life. Once he or she has learned to talk, be prepared for questions day and night. Curiosity is part of this child's nature, but it is a positive characteristic and should certainly not be ignored. Fobbing off Scorpios with insufficient information is useless, especially as it will only make them even more curious.

Whilst your Scorpio child may apparently be loving and extrovert, there is also a very private side to his or her personality, and if sharing a bedroom with other children in your family is a necessity, try to allocate a separate little space which can be his or her very own. It will be really appreciated and will show you do understand this special need.

The curious nature of Scorpions often makes them experiment and, of course, not every experiment is desirable. It is true to say that many people born under this sign can all too easily become prey to negative influences in later years, which may also include alcohol, drugs and bad company. Therefore as a parent, your guidance is just what is needed. Scorpio is not a weak sign, and you will soon realize that your child can combine gentleness and love with a great deal of strength and self-control.

The first years

SAGITTARIUS

It has often been said that Sagittarians are clowns at heart, and when you take your first look at your very own infant, you can almost imagine that little mouth with a joke on its lips. However, comedy often goes hand in hand with pathos, and a clown's white face and bright red lips may sometimes be a cover-up for sadness. Don't start to think that just because you have always read that Sagittarian children are happy-go-lucky little souls, your offspring is not going to need just as much care and attention as every child needs because you would be wrong.

It *is* true that Sagittarians *are* happy-go-lucky a great deal of the time, but there is more to them than that. Your Sagittarian child will cry just as loudly as Leo, Pisces and everyone else if something is wrong, and Sagittarian tears are no less important even if you do soon discover they are often followed five minutes later by a beaming smile.

Sagittarius is the last of the Fire signs, following on from Aries and Leo. It is Mutable and Positive, all of which basically means that Sagittarians are energetic, and are good at expressing and asserting themselves, plus having the ability to adapt to each and every environment. The symbol of Sagittarius is the Centaur, who is half man and half horse, carrying a bow and arrow, and both mentally and physically this sign is the explorer of the Zodiac. The further that arrow can be aimed, the happier Sagittarius will be.

It will not be long before you realize that almost as soon as a Sagittarian learns to move those little limbs the urge to explore with a capital E will predominate your child's mind and you are certainly going to have your hands full. However, don't start imagining that you are going to need a cot with extra high sides or will necessarily soon have to lock every door that leads to the outside world. It is simply a question of making it very clear who is the boss from the start.

You will soon be immensely proud of your child's enquiring mind and thirst for knowledge. Sagittarius is called "the Sage and Counsellor of the Zodiac", and if you can teach your little Sagittarian how to get on with other children so that he or she doesn't start showing off there will be a great deal of mutual respect between you.

I usually hate to hear the word "luck" used in connection with astrology, but I do feel that to have Jupiter as a ruler is definitely a blessing. In mythology, the Romans thought of Jupiter as the most powerful of all the Gods, and a protector of justice and virtue. Sagittarians on the whole do tend to be lucky, and you will start to realize this once there is a Sagittarius in your family.

Healthwise, the most sensitive areas for Sagittarius are the hips, lungs, thighs, and sciatic nerves. All children are prone to childhood illnesses, but Sagittarians usually recover quickly. However Sagittarians can be almost as accident prone as Ariens, with a dare-devil attitude to life which may prove to be a problem. This is where your guidance and discipline is going to be invaluable, because whilst cosseting your child would be wrong, it would also be a mistake to let him or her develop the inherent desire for freedom at too early an age.

A Sagittarian loves company, and even when very small will soon make it apparent that he or she doesn't like to be left alone for long. There is sometimes a strange mixture in Sagittarius – an urge for freedom and yet an often undeniable need to be part of the family, as long as it is on Sagittarius' terms. As a parent you will be expected to cater to both these desires, and it is obviously up to you as to how you behave. Just remember it will be your influence which is going to help your Sagittarian grow up in a positive way, which means explaining that a desire for freedom could turn into selfishness, and that to be really popular it is important also to fit in with other people's plans and not insist always on having things one's own way.

The first years

CAPRICORN

I feel that the phrase "an old head on young shoulders" must have been invented specifically for children born between December 23 and January 20.

The symbol of Capricorn is based on that of a goat with a curling fish's tail, who was called Capricornus by the ancient Chaldeans, but today this astrological symbol is usually described as a mountain goat, and it is often true that people born under Capricorn tackle life rather like an ascent up a steep mountain full of crags and potholes, but nevertheless, determinedly reach the top. Capricorn is a Cardinal Earth and Negative sign, and people born under this sign tend to be prudent and disciplined.

You will soon discover that your Capricorn baby is actually not a "baby" in the true sense of the word. You will instinctively realize from your newborn infant's face that he or she sees life as a serious business. This is where your love and guidance will be invaluable in setting the right pattern for the future.

Nappy changes and feeding times can often cause real scenes with children of other signs, but if you follow a set routine they can run much more smoothly with a Capricorn.

However, remember that Capricorn can sometimes lose out on a great deal of happiness by being too serious at too early an age. Even if it does make life easier for you to have a child who is as good as gold, it would be helping that same child much more if he or she can grow up in a happy-go-lucky atmosphere of laughter and smiling faces. Your child needs to develop a sense of humour, to learn that muddy knees will not necessarily mean punishment. It is important to encourage your child to have playmates of the same age, instead of preferring adult company. Emotional security is of course important to all children, but it is

especially so to a Capricorn, and although your child may not seem outwardly sensitive, he or she will soon be aware of family problems no matter how hard you try to keep them hidden.

People born under the sign of Capricorn may suffer from skin rashes and disorders, and knee and bone troubles, whilst holding back their emotions or eating incorrectly can sometimes lead to digestive problems. You may find that your Capricorn child suffers more than some of the other signs with childhood illnesses, but once these are past, he or she often leads an even healthier life than some of the other signs. I remember reading once that Capricorn subjects are rather like good wines because they both improve with age, and I can think of several elderly Capricorns who bear out this point exceptionally well. If, therefore, your child doesn't seem to be as healthy as other children and your doctor sees no cause for worry, it could simply be this Capricorn influence. However, once again your guidance in pointing out the benefits of sufficient exercise, sunshine and fresh air will be invaluable. You shouldn't have to fuss over your child unnecessarily, although with the Capricorn tendency to have bone weaknesses, you may have to be prepared to cope with a few twists and sprains.

Learn to understand your child from the beginning and encourage a positive attitude to life, because it is far too easy for him or her to become narrow-minded and melancholy, whilst a misunderstood Capricorn can sometimes develop selfish or even unkind characteristics. Material possessions always seem to matter a great deal to this sign, but love and laughter will be more valuable as gifts to your Capricorn child than the most expensive toy ever could be.

The first years

AQUARIUS

I certainly don't wish to imply that Aquarians are more likely to be trouble makers than anyone else, but if you have just become the parent of an Aquarian child, don't expect your life to run smoothly, for Aquarians are the most unpredictable of all the signs. However, if you ever try to point this out to someone born between January 20 and February 18 you might well be reminded that Aquarius is also known as the sign of "genius".

Naturally your infant isn't likely to start calculating logarithms or fathoming out just how electricity works, but it won't be long before you realize that apart from being interested in everyone and everything, your child also possesses a great deal of intuition.

Aquarius is often misunderstood because people think it is a Water sign, its symbol being "The Water Bearer or Water Carrier". However, Aquarius is an Air sign, and although the symbol resembles ripples of water, it could also represent waves of electricity. Aquarius is a Fixed Positive sign, which basically means Aquarians are communicative, mentally active and intense, but also unconventional.

You will soon discover that your child makes his or her presence felt, and one of the most important factors in bringing up an Aquarian is to establish a rapport from the start. Remember that Aquarius is an intellectual sign, and even a toddler will resent "baby" language. You may also discover that your child can almost read your mind before you have had a chance to say what you are thinking.

As an Aquarian child's personality may have a stubborn side, it is extremely important that this negative characteristic is dealt with when young. Aquarians need to feel inwardly free, but unless you become adept at explaining the reasons

44

for self-control you could end up with a rebellious teenager on your hands.

It is often difficult for Aquarians to show their feelings outwardly, and although affectionate by nature, they may be unlikely to smother you with hugs and kisses. However, your child must be taught that love should not be hidden away, but expressed. It may not always be simple to give advice to an Aquarian child but you should persevere.

Aquarians can have circulation problems and may be prone to bumps and bruises and twists and sprains, especially around the ankles which tend to be weak. As an Aquarian's mind is always busy, a healthy way of life, plus sufficient sleep are important from childhood.

Your Aquarian child will soon make it obvious that play-mates are a major necessity, but you may discover that they are more likely to be casual friends than really close ones, and this pattern is likely to continue. Never try and force your child into mixing with the children you prefer, because you will be accused of being prejudiced or interfering. Your child has a unique ability to get on with people from all walks of life, and this should be encouraged unless you see it leading to problems.

Even when quite small you will discover your little Aquarian is not only perceptive but is highly sensitive to atmosphere, so don't try to hide your feelings or any problems from your child.

The first years

PISCES

When you first gaze at your child sleeping peacefully, or greeting you with a smile, and you recall other screaming, scowling babies in the past, you will be delighted that yours was born under the sign of Pisces.

45

Your child could be a joy to bring up, but a great deal will depend on you. Pisces is the most impressionable, emotional, sensitive and intuitive of all the Zodiacal signs. The most important factor for you to realize is that you have brought the original dreamer into the world, and whilst dreams are marvellous in the right place, your child must certainly not grow up in a fantasy world over-protected from unpleasant realities.

You will also have to remember the famous Piscean intuition, for your child will soon learn exactly how to charm you into passive obedience. Pisceans are good at emotional blackmail even when very young, and it is amazing how many parents can be deceived by this.

Pisceans of every age will react immediately if treated unjustly, and because of your child's sensitivity, it is vitally important that you do not raise your voice unnecessarily.

Pisces is a Water sign, Mutable and Negative, which basically means Pisceans are passive, emotional, with intuitive qualities. The symbol of Pisces represents two fish joined together but pulling in opposite directions, which would seem to represent the dual and vacillating nature of Pisceans. The planetary ruler of Pisces is Neptune, who in mythology was Neptunus, the God of the Sea to the Romans, and Poseidon to the Greeks. Pisces is also said to be influenced by the planet Jupiter, but it is Neptune's influence which gives Pisceans their inspirational and yet unworldly qualities.

Your Piscean child will not only be loving but will also seem to understand your every mood. If you are feeling sad, your child's eyes may start to fill with tears; there will be an empathy between you and your son or daughter almost from the moment he or she is born.

Even if you have a busy life yourself and feel exhausted when it is time to put your child to bed, never neglect that bed-time story you may have promised earlier in the day, because these quiet moments with you before going to sleep are very important.

Try not to be overly protective towards your child, as a Piscean must learn to stand alone rather than always rely on someone else to make all the decisions. Love and understanding should be combined with discipline which, whilst not being too severe, should certainly be realistic. Remember too that Pisceans are often basically shy, so don't force your child to be the centre of attention when the situation is becoming embarrassing. Many Pisceans are born actors and mimics, and if your child does want to be in the limelight, he or she won't need any encouraging.

Pisceans do sometimes distort the truth to suit themselves, mainly because they live in their own little make-believe world. Naturally this doesn't mean that all of them grow up to be uncontrollable liars, but some of the stories you are told may have deviated from the truth, and you must impress upon your child early on that it is always important to be truthful.

Pisceans are sometimes not as strong as the other signs, and colds can turn too easily into something more serious, so your infant may need more care and attention during childhood. Whilst it would be wrong to fuss unnecessarily, make sure your child is wrapped up warmly when chill winds are blowing outside. Pisceans are also inclined to suffer with foot problems, so make sure you buy properly fitting shoes. They are so emotional they can also be prone to nervous stress.

The greatest gift you can give to a Piscean baby is a happy household where love and understanding are the order of the day. In return you will be blessed with someone whose own compassion and devotion will grow with the years.

THE EARLY YEARS

... *growing up*

Growing up can be a great deal of fun but it can also be extremely difficult at times. Do you remember your first day of school when perhaps the sight of hundreds of other children terrified you? Or did you immediately start to chatter away and make new friends? The headmaster or mistress of the school may have asked a great many questions, but it is unlikely that they asked either your parents or yourself which star sign you were born under. Perhaps your own growing up could have been made easier if that had taken place.

Psychiatrists tend to go back to events that happened in their patient's childhood and adolescence in order to make a true definition. I would never dream of arguing case histories with a psychiatrist, I would simply like to add that perhaps if more of them, and indeed more doctors too, also made a study of astrology, it might astound them with its accuracy and help them to understand their patients even more.

Growing up is an especially important phase in our lives. In many ways our behaviour pattern is set very early on, and we are motivated into doing things a certain way, perhaps from our first days at school. It may not be all that long ago that you looked on with admiration and envy whilst a nine-year-old boy was being praised in front of the whole class for having top marks yet again. You might have felt better if you had discovered he was a Capricorn who, even at that age, felt that working hard was the only way to get on in the world. However, perhaps his parents could also have helped him more if they had let him know that even Capricorns should find some time to have fun and games. Even if that boy is now a hard-working twenty-five-year-old in a responsible position, perhaps he missed out on entertainment along the way.

I would like to give you an insight into these important years for the children of each sign, to enable you to watch them grow into adolescence and adulthood with a positive and optimistic approach to the life which is ahead of them. I also want to help you be aware of particular pitfalls which may arise and suggest some constructive ways in which to deal with them.

Some adults are always children at heart, so even if you don't have children of your own, you might find some of the information contained in this part of the book equally applicable to you!

Growing up

ARIES

The growing-up years are vitally important for all children, and as Ariens absorb everything, have a hundred and one interests and a never-ending amount of energy, together with a great vitality and enthusiasm for life, it can sometimes be exhausting for everyone else. However, it can also be fun.

The early years are the time to teach your child that patience is a virtue and not simply a bore. Life will be so much easier once he or she understands that the world wasn't made for Aries alone. There are some Ariens who never do learn this and they wonder why they are sometimes unpopular.

Having got through infancy with the usual childhood ailments and perhaps a few inevitable bumps and bruises, is your child now able to combat his or her headstrong impulses to face the world as if it were a battlefield?

An Aries child may not be as stubborn or moody as some children of other signs, but if you want good results on school reports, remember that low marks do not necessarily mean lack of brains, but could also be because of lack of interest and motivation, and if boredom takes over from your child's initial enthusiasm, the Aries mind will wander.

This is where a "challenge" can come in useful. Having previously said that it's not right to look on life as a battle-field, one way to get your Aries child through school and the various stages of growing up is sometimes to admire openly another child's progress, perhaps showing that you feel your own offspring doesn't quite match up to this. However, this should never be done in a heavy-handed way, especially if your child is easily upset, but on the positive side it could inspire your child to show you just how clever he or she can be, even if it means forgetting about playtime and "burning the midnight oil" for a few weeks.

Always remember that some children are especially sensitive to atmosphere and ambience, and if there are any problems between you and your partner, it is often far better to let your child realize this as gently as possible, and obviously, at an age where it is not too difficult for them to understand, especially as Ariens are basically frank and honest, and they detest lies from other people.

Growing up can be exciting for an Arien child, but some-times an independent air continues to go hand in hand with a certain amount of vulnerability and need for praise and admiration.

"Encouragement" is perhaps one of the words most neces-sary in the growing-up stages of an Aries child. Even great leaders were children once, and don't you suppose they received encouragement themselves?

Whilst your child is growing up, it is the right time to encourage his or her qualities of honesty, enthusiasm, energy and idealism, but also to teach the importance of keeping in check a quick temper, an aggressive manner, headstrong ways and a sometimes over-confident ego.

In some ways Ariens never do grow up completely. Their particular brand of childlike wonder and interest in life can be marvellously refreshing to people when they feel jaded and disillusioned. Always try to make sure, however, that you impress upon your child the importance of allowing his or her action-packed brain to have sufficient rest and relaxation, for once this is understood it should help to make life easier for everybody.

Growing up
TAURUS

Your Taurus child should have learnt by now that there are certain rules in life which must be obeyed by everyone, and provided you have given satisfactory explanations for these, there should be no problems.

However, growing up also means leaving the nest and moving away from that safe environment called home. Parents won't always be present to look after their offspring if any difficulties arise, and other people aren't always so willing to give explanations for their demands.

The first day of school could be tricky for many children, and although your little Taurean may not be excessively shy, he or she could react rather slowly when surrounded by lots of new people. Once you have made your choice of school therefore it might be wise to make sure your child has at least visited it and met the teachers, so that the newness of everything won't be quite so overwhelming. Don't expect to be greeted with a display of great enthusiasm at the end of the first day, for it's going to take a while before your Taurean child has summed things up sufficiently to tell you exactly what he or she has thought, but when you do hear, it will be a truthful picture.

Don't be surprised if the first term's report shows steady progress rather than any brilliant marks, for that is the Taurus personality – "steady", but certainly hardworking. You should not be let down when it's time for him or her to sit for important exams. Taureans may not necessarily thrive on challenges, but they certainly appreciate the value of education, and nothing will stop them from putting their best effort in to achieve results which will make you proud of them.

During the growing up years, if your child doesn't want to mix with certain people, or to play certain games, it might need more than rational explanations to convince him or her that learning to get on with other people is important. Always remember, however, to combine discipline with love, for without affection, children can develop a hard and bitter edge, and you certainly don't want your child to turn into a dictator as some Taureans have done in history.

Growing up is also a time when Taurean children who have felt unhappy at home may start to grow a protective "shell" around themselves. Unfortunately this shell can also be interpreted by other people as obstinacy, when it may simply be pure defence.

A Taurean child needs people to understand his or her inner feelings. Taureans may not be the dreamers of the Zodiac but they certainly have ideals, so it's vitally important to find out what is really going on in your child's mind and to learn the reasons for his or her likes and dislikes.

Emotional security will always be of major importance, especially during these years, because this is often when Taureans start to plan their futures, even if only sub-consciously. Childhood impressions are not usually forgotten, and can influence the rest of their lives.

Taureans usually find it easy to understand the value of money, and are not extravagant. You won't often have pocket money problems with your child.

· However, your child should be encouraged to exercise, as Taureans can be lazy, and prefer to potter around in a garden than indulge in sports. Unfortunately they also tend to put on weight easily, and lack of exercise combined with a love of food can wreak havoc on a young body.

Make sure your Taurean youngster doesn't become too self-indulgent, or too possessive with his or her particular friends, and encourage any creative talents which may be developing. A Taurean who doesn't like music often has some other artistic interest.

Let your Taurus child realize that dreams and aspirations can all come true, and that making the most of a potential can be better than following in someone else's footsteps.

A Taurean may not be guilty of saying "it can't be done", but can be inclined to say "I don't want to" or "I just don't feel like it", and these are attitudes which, if carried over into adult life, can make a person seem dull. Point out, therefore, that being more adaptable and open-minded will be a positive characteristic to practise whilst growing up.

Growing up

GEMINI

Geminians are rather like Ariens in the respect that they want to be everywhere, see everything, do everything, all in the shortest possible time. However, one important difference is that a typical Gemini can dissipate his or her nervous energies even faster than an Arien, by cramming everything haphazardly into the day without rhyme or reason, achieving very little.

It is vitally important to impress upon the young Geminian that having some kind of direction in life isn't a boring waste of time, but is actually essential and very positive. You don't want your particular offspring to end

up drifting from one job to another, from one person to another, for ever.

Children often rebel against parents, other family influences, and school, around the ages of thirteen or fourteen, and this could especially apply to a Gemini who, being the butterfly of the Zodiac, feels a sudden urge to be free.

As this sign is definitely involved with mental communication, giving your Gemini child love and affection without understanding what is going on in his or her mind will be of little use. You must try and learn to understand his thoughts and ideas, which may be thrown in your direction at an unbelievably fast rate. Hopefully, you really did arm yourself with dictionaries and encyclopaedias when your child was small, and if not you'd better rectify that mistake now!

Start subscribing to magazines in the right age-range, and make sure there are soft drinks in the refrigerator for when schoolfriends come to play. Gemini is a sociable sign, and the importance of friendship should be taught, although your child should also be encouraged to cherish friends and not drop them just because someone or something more interesting seems to have come along, for a negative characteristic of Gemini seems to be the conviction that life is better on the other side of the fence. Perhaps this would be the right moment to point out to your child that continual searching for new fields can lead to eventual disappointment, especially as a Geminian often doesn't know what he or she is searching for.

Gemini children tend to be bright, chatty and wonderfully positive in their attitude to life, which is why it is so important that although their minds should be free to wander, it is also vital for them to learn to concentrate on just one thing at a time.

These children tend to be quick at learning, but can be equally quick to forget because of their insistence of moving on to the next lesson. Languages often come easily, so encourage your child to learn foreign tongues as early as possible.

Growing up is an important time in everyone's life, because it sets the pattern for the future. One lovely characteristic of Geminians is that, like Peter Pan, they never completely grow up, seeming to retain a youthful air and brisk step for ever. If their restlessness can be controlled, their inquisitive manner put to good use so that they don't become gossips, and their clever little brains exercised in the most productive ways, you should certainly be proud of your Gemini child.

Two friends of mine certainly went about this in a positive way. Their seventeen-year-old son has all the characteristics of the typical Gemini, bright, inquisitive, asking questions almost as soon as he was able to talk. True to form he went through a slightly difficult time when he was about thirteen, but his parents continued to listen to his views, to encourage him at school, to let him take a job in the holidays so that he could feel independent. He passed all his school exams with flying colours, and when I last saw his father and enquired about him, I was told proudly that the boy had just started working in his own business.

No one is asking you to treat an eleven or twelve year old child as you would an adult, but always remember that a great deal depends on the right kind of communication when you are the parent of a Gemini son or daughter.

Growing up

CANCER

By now your child should have learnt that there is an interesting world outside the home, and that it is important to learn how to mix with other people, because this will certainly be necessary at school. Your child should also have realized by now that although it is wonderful to have loving

parents, it is also necessary to be independent too. He or she may feel miserable the first time you wave goodbye at a school entrance, but if you are overly protective you could do more harm than good.

Your child may still at times be shy, but can soon become a chattering little magpie amongst newfound friends. Cancerians tend to have wonderfully retentive memories, and schooldays give them the chance to prove just how bright they can be. After the first history lesson you may have everything repeated to you almost verbatim!

Growing up can be a difficult time for everyone, and for a Cancerian it may be especially so because of the sensitive and sentimental characteristics of this sign. Understanding your child's emotions is therefore highly important, although it doesn't mean you have to agree with everything all the time, for a Cancerian can also be stubborn. Sometimes his or her moods may be an excuse to avoid listening to reason, and if your child should become accustomed to having everything his or her own way, it will come as a shock when friends and colleagues in later years turn a deaf ear to moans and laments. Remember, however, that being teased can be an agonizing experience, even though it can often be an integral part of growing up.

Whilst the parents of a Gemini child need to understand the importance of communication, for a Cancerian child the most appropriate word is probably "empathy"; understanding how your child feels and trying to relate to him or her in the best possible way.

If a Cancerian child grows up as a misfit or rebel, it can often be because he or she has been misunderstood very early on. It sounds very easy to put the blame on other people, but the basic characteristics of a Cancerian are such that with the right kind of understanding, it shouldn't be difficult for your child to find an appropriate niche in life.

Whereas so many children seem to rebel against the family influence once they reach their teens, your Cancerian child may almost become closer to you, tends always to remember

special anniversaries, and is usually especially helpful around the home. In the school holidays your child may want to take a part-time job, perhaps delivering papers, or taking on some extra housework in order to earn a little more pocket money. Don't worry too much about your child becoming extravagant, because he or she will soon understand the necessity and importance of money.

Depending on your own behaviour and attitude, to have a Cancerian child growing up in your home can be fun for everyone, providing you never forget that you have brought a sensitive soul into the world and that harsh words used unfairly will cause a great deal of hurt.

If your child shows artistic and creative talent, always give lots of encouragement, as this will help overcome any feelings of insecurity.

Your son or daughter will probably react to atmosphere more than children of other signs, and if you also happen to be a Cancerian you will certainly understand those sudden changes of mood, that deep inner yearning for security, blended with daydreams.

However, no matter what sign *you* were born under, always remember that the right amount of love and understanding, coupled with a sense of humour and a genuine interest in watching and helping your child to grow up, will all be a positive aid and a constructive send off into the adult world.

Growing up
LEO

If your child has hitherto shown none of those dominating qualities which astrologers always ascribe to Leo, and has been docile and obedient most of the time, then his or her personal horoscope must be greatly influenced by the Ascendant based on the exact time of birth and various planetary aspects, or perhaps it's simply that these qualities haven't had a chance to show yet!

The childhood years for a Leo are especially important because the way your child behaves will set a pattern for the future. As your child grows up, the extrovert Leo personality will start to show more and more. In one way or another, but especially at school, he or she is going to make you sit up and take notice.

A Leo child can far too easily turn into a show-off if you don't point out early on that other people soon get bored with this type of behaviour, but although you must be firm with your discipline, don't ever forget to hand it out in a warm and loving way.

Luckily your child is unlikely to be a bully with other children. Even the most domineering and bossy little Leo usually possesses an inner sense of fair play and your child will always have a soft spot when it comes to dealing with less fortunate people.

Once your Leo child is no longer a baby you will have to be fairly tough when it comes to tidying up and helping around the house. Although Leos have so much natural energy and vitality, you may be surprised to learn they can also be unbelievably lazy. Perhaps this stems from feeling superior, and expecting everyone else to clear up after them, but as a parent you'd better make sure you don't put up with it, because you will only be doing your child a disservice. In the future, your son or daughter may have to learn the hard way that no one is going to help them until they've learned to do things for themselves, and the younger that lesson is learnt the better. Be prepared for a house full of friends, for moods which can sometimes fluctuate almost as much as a Cancerian's, for practical jokes, pop music blaring, and a great deal of activity going on around you.

Your child is likely to have a natural flair for acting. The sign of Leo rules the fifth house in the Zodiac, which relates to the house of children, love affairs and also creativity. Many Leos gravitate towards the world of show business as they get older, and watching your own Leo grow up you will soon understand why.

Leo has to be a star, which is why it is so important for you to be around to make sure that success at school, in sport, in competitions, in exams, doesn't start to make your child conceited. Leo likes to be not only a leader, but also a winner — and when your child is striving for something important you won't see any of the signs of laziness or tiredness which tend to appear when there are jobs to do around the house.

If your Leo has been an only child, and suddenly you have a new baby to take care of, do make sure your Leo doesn't feel threatened. Let him or her feel confident that your love is not going to diminish in any way. Just because of an outwardly confident exterior, parents sometimes think their child is inwardly confident too, but the growing up years are a time when many children are especially vulnerable, and your Leo may be too.

You may have to be especially firm about pocket money. It is wonderful to have a kind-hearted and generous child, but you probably can't afford to treat the rest of the neighbourhood, and this could easily happen unless the value of money is understood and appreciated.

Try to ensure that your home surroundings are bright and comfortable. Your child thrives in a happy environment, but should there be a break-up in the family, let him or her be aware of what is going on. It really would be a case of wounded Leo pride if you calmly went about re-organizing your own life, leaving it till the last minute to tell your child, especially as Leos tend to have great strength of mind and like being treated as adults early on.

If you can imagine a bear with a sore head, that is how I can visualize a Leo who feels unloved, and a Leo child who grows up in an atmosphere of love, without being spoilt or fussed over, will become an adult you will be proud of.

Growing up

VIRGO

One of the marvellous things about a Virgo child is that there should be no punctuality problems, for whether getting up in the morning, arriving for meals, or even going to school, it is almost as if Virgo has an inbuilt clock which sounds off an alarm at the appropriate time.

You shouldn't have much trouble encouraging your child to study at school either. An inborn ability to sit quietly and concentrate will prove a boon in future years, and should mean that when it comes to exam time everything will be smooth sailing. You must, however, remember that Virgo is often a worrier at heart, and that the best way to overcome this is to be sure to give your child extra encouragement and advice.

It may not necessarily be good for your child to pore over text books for hours without spending at least a short time in the fresh air, but a Virgo child may need a great deal of convincing about this. A quiet Virgo is unlikely to turn into an extrovert overnight, but it certainly wouldn't hurt him or her to have a little more fun. You must try and get your child to discuss problems with you. It is extremely necessary for a Virgo to understand the importance of talking more. You don't want your child to become an introvert, bottling up feelings and getting a reputation of being cold and unemotional, when the truth of the matter is that he or she is simply so used to holding back that it becomes incredibly difficult to behave in any other way.

However, while a Virgo child is not likely to be as restless as the other Mercury ruled sign, Gemini, there can be an independent, adventurous side to his or her nature too.

Virgo is a perfectionist, and while your child is growing up it would be wonderful if you could help him or her to realize that sometimes by searching desperately for perfection, it is easy to miss out on a great deal. I think that Hermann Hesse's "Siddhartha" should be compulsory reading for a young Virgo. Remembered as a "cult" book for past hippie generations, there is still a great deal for a typical Virgo to learn from its message.

Your child may want you to know about how badly behaved the neighbour's child across the street was at school the other day, or what a ridiculous dress one of the teachers was wearing, but if you start to criticize him or her along the same lines, you may get an indignant reply. A Virgo child should be made to realize that someone who goes through life pointing out defects in other people is not going to be very popular if he or she can't accept similar criticism. It is important to encourage your child to have a broader outlook on life, and to see both sides of an argument. Perhaps you should make sure there are a few Libran children around, although Libra's weighing and balancing of ideas could make a Virgo irritated!

If you are prepared to work at understanding your child, especially in the adolescent years, when Virgo's somewhat shy and reticent air could make it difficult for him or her to talk to you about the every-day problems of growing up, you will be doing your child a great service. Remember how much your child needs your affection, even though it may not show. It is going to have a great bearing on the way relationships turn out in later years.

Break-ups in the family can be difficult for a Virgo to accept. That is why it is important to encourage every member of the family to talk openly to each other. As long as your child realizes he or she is not going to lose out it will all be much easier. Virgo doesn't always have to be the star of the show, but not to have your feelings considered is hurtful whatever the age.

Your child may not grow up a great outdoor or sports lover, or an extrovert speaker, but if you encourage the talents you discover, and also encourage the sense of humour which is often lurking below the surface of a somewhat self-conscious personality, you will be helping your child to find the right niche in the adult world.

Growing up
LIBRA

Have you pointed out the whys and wherefores of everything? Have you carefully tried to guide your Libran child along the right path, avoiding losing your temper when he or she took ages to decide whether it was better to go and play with the neighbour's children, or to stay in to practise the piano? Hopefully your child will now have learned the importance of making decisions.

Once the time arrives for your child to start school, a part of the training will be out of your hands. This doesn't mean, however, that you will become any less important. Schooldays may be fun, but a happy and settled family life is necessary too. You'd better start reading up on facts and figures forgotten long ago. Your Libran child is likely to be bright, will assimilate information easily, and have an enquiring mind. Do you remember how he or she used to bring home those unwanted pets? Pretty soon you are going to have to find the answer to the question why there is so much injustice in the world. Your Libran child will hate to think that privileges exist where they should not. This Libran sense of fair play will show more and more whilst your child is growing, and although he or she may not necessarily be able to find acceptable alternatives to the things they find wrong – it is you who will be expected to come up with ideal solutions.

Colour and sound were probably always important to your child, and whilst he or she is growing up you could easily find that, in common with many others born under this sign, your little Libran is very creative. You should certainly offer as much encouragement as you can, but also remember that not everyone is going to turn into a musical or artistic genius.

Whilst encouraging the creative talents of your child, it is of paramount importance that outdoor life is not neglected. It is often a Libran habit to curl up with an interesting book, or listen to a favourite record, instead of dressing up warmly and braving a chilly wintry day. Likewise, your child may prefer watching school friends play a game of tennis to making the physical effort of joining in.

Once it comes to pocket money time, your guidance will be especially invaluable. Perhaps Venus should be blamed for the desire to be surrounded by beautiful things. However, your child from an early age tends to want the best, for Libra is not only an idealist, but may be almost as much of a perfectionist as Virgo. It will definitely be up to you to try and teach him or her the value of money. A money box could help, but the rational explanation of *why* it is important to learn to save will be more helpful still.

Your child should be encouraged to mix with other children as much as possible, for sometimes lazy moods prevent him or her from making the effort, and yet Librans do tend to thrive in company.

As you watch your child grow up, you may notice how easy it is for him or her to charm other people, and you will be delighted to realize that diplomacy and tact seem to be an inherent part of the Libran personality. However, you must ensure that your child doesn't start to become vain, or develop unnecessarily exotic tastes in food.

Your child may be a delight a great deal of the time, but there will also be moments when the lazy or the argumentative side to his or her nature will need an abundance of understanding.

Librans may not be as moody as some Cancerians, but they can have their ups and downs, and as a parent you can be invaluable in making the "downs" appear less often than the "ups". It may be easy for your child to be popular, but it is the love and approval of an immediate family which is the most important factor, so never forget this.

Growing up

SCORPIO

Whilst your child is growing up, life will become even more fascinating to him or her. There is so much to see and to learn about, and your Scorpio boy or girl won't miss a thing.

If you gave your child the necessary guidance whilst still very young, then it shouldn't be difficult to continue along the same lines now.

However, once it comes to school-time, you obviously won't be able to know everything that is going on during the day, and if your child should get in with the wrong set of friends it is then that the trouble could start. For someone as perceptive as a Scorpio, it is amazing that they can so easily be persuaded to flirt with danger and experiment with negative ways of living. A Scorpio with his or her interest in discovering what life is all about, probably can't help having strong sexual curiosity which might easily show earlier than in children born under other signs, so wise sex education at the right age is most important.

Your Scorpio has a bright mind and will be an avid learner, provided he or she has respect for the teachers. Facts and figures usually present no problems for Scorpio, and biology, chemistry, science, and physics will often be especially fascinating to both boys and girls. Your child could also excel at sports, and physical exercise is good for Scorpio because of that power house of energy burning away inside, but do remember that this sign can sometimes take too many risks and is attracted to anything dangerous.

You will often discover that your child tends to see things either in black or in white. He or she will either "hate" or "love" and it is important to try to encourage Scorpio to realize that so passionately dividing life into two divisions can create enormous problems.

I have often felt that "playing with fire" was a phrase invented especially with Scorpios in mind, which takes on a different meaning however when it is implied to events in every-day life. Whilst young, your child may be too fascinated by matches and the gas stoves. I also mentioned drugs in an earlier chapter, and although I don't want to be repetitive I feel it is imperative for you to realize that a Scorpio child with a desire to discover the secrets of life and death, can sometimes, more than children born under other signs, be led in the wrong direction. This curiosity to get to the root of things is part of what makes Scorpio such an intriguing, interesting person but as an adolescent, curiosity must be balanced by solid parental guidance. Religion can also be fascinating to Scorpio, and there is a strong spiritual side to this sign.

Whilst growing up, your Scorpio child may demonstrate more and more the need for privacy, and if a separate bed-room is still impossible, don't forget he or she needs to have a special little space of his own.

Lead your child along a positive path. Try to make him or her understand that it is not always possible to be treated fairly in the world, but that revenge is a negative reaction. A Scorpio can be cruel, but is often emotionally very insecure, yet once a Scorpio believes in you, you couldn't hope for more loyalty from anyone.

Adolescence is a difficult stage in your child's life, and for Scorpio it is vital that there are people around who will take the time to explain about life and the problems that may be encountered whilst growing up. You will never regret the efforts you make in helping your child to be successful, and will often have a great deal to be proud of.

Growing up

SAGITTARIUS

Sagittarius rules the ninth house of the Zodiac, which relates to long distance travel and to what is known as "the higher mind". Once your child starts school, you will soon discover that a Sagittarian's thirst for knowledge will embrace every conceivable subject. However, never forget your child may also be restless, and needs to be taught the importance of concentration early on.

As your child grows up, you will discover with pleasure that you usually get a truthful answer to everything you ask, perhaps sometimes too truthful, because if you ask your eleven year old daughter if she thinks you look good in your new suit, she might tell you straight out that you have developed a few bulges which were not there a few weeks ago. Honesty is a positive virtue, but so is diplomacy, and you will probably find you need to teach your child the virtue of being tactful. I can think of several adult Sagittarians who are capable of deflating someone's happy mood by being too frank.

Your Sagittarian child is unlikely to have much difficulty making friends with other children, in fact your home may be filled with playmates almost as soon as your child starts to walk. A Sagittarian needs company, and if yours is an only child, or you are a one parent family, do make every effort to make sure that there are playmates around. As a parent you may find yourself worrying as your son or daughter is likely to be one of those children who tend to come home late from wherever they may have been. The most important factor to remember is that once you have accepted that your child is by nature honest, you must learn to trust this honesty, otherwise you will be doing your child a great disservice. A Sagittarian child can never be tied to a mother's apron strings, even if the strings *are* invisible, and forcing him or her to do something without a valid reason is bound to produce arguments which might even be justified. Thoreau once wrote "I was not born to be forced. I will breathe after my own fashion ... If a plant cannot live according to its nature, it dies; and so a man". If you are beginning to think that Sagittarian babies grow up into selfish inconsiderate teenagers, then you are on the wrong track. Sagittarians are not selfish, but sometimes think their knowledge is greater than yours – once there is mutual respect between you there will be a much better relationship.

If your child is not interested in sport or an outdoor life, it will be most unusual, and must mean that other planetary aspects are influencing the Sagittarius Sun, which tends to give people born under this sign a great love of activity. If your child is very active, encourage this, but try to point out that being reckless could lead to unnecessary accidents.

Many Sagittarians are drawn to religion and philosophy, and your child may be fascinated more by bible stories than others. Once again, there is often a contrast between the energetic outgoing and jokey child, and the serious thinker who wants to learn more about what lies beyond our immediate horizons.

Sagittarius is often so busy discovering the world that mealtimes are forgotten, so it is up to you to point out the importance of eating regularly and correctly, and to see that your child turns up at the table on time, for otherwise you probably won't see him or her! It will also be up to you to teach your Sagittarian the value of money, which won't be easy, but is of great importance because Sagittarians can turn into gamblers far too easily.

A household where everyone is informal and open with each other, where at least one pet is welcome, and where your child can grow up in a healthy atmosphere, will contribute a vital part to your Sagittarian's adult life.

Growing up
CAPRICORN

Have you endeavoured to show your Capricorn child that even though the media may continually remind us of all the negative aspects of the world we live in, a Capricorn with an optimistic and positive approach to life will have a head start in dealing with adversity?

Once it is time to go to school, your child will start to become even more organized and responsible. Studying doesn't usually present many problems for a Capricorn and in fact it may be more difficult to convince your child to close school books in order to eat or play, than to persuade him or her to learn French verbs. You'd better remember that Saturn's influence means your child may not be incredibly quick at learning, but there certainly shouldn't be any need to worry because he or she almost always makes up for lost time. Being top of the class or passing exams with high marks come naturally to people born under this sign. Capricorns love power, but it must not be allowed to go to their heads. Don't let your child become so ambitious and strong-willed that he or she starts dominating not only other children, but you as well.

A Capricorn child's respect for age and wisdom means it is necessary for him or her not only to love you as a parent but also to admire you. Should there be any problems within your immediate family circle, or even separation or divorce, never let your child feel neglected. It is important that he or she understands what is going on and the reasons for it. Apart from anything else, your Capricorn child will prove to be not only a loving son or daughter, but also a true friend.

If you have a large family, you may have discovered by now that your Capricorn is marvellous at looking after other children, and that you can delegate with confidence some of the responsibility for their welfare to your teenager. This is especially useful if you have a job and spend quite a lot of time away from the home.

However, the adolescent years can be difficult for many children, and especially for Capricorn, as Saturn's influence sometimes creates a tendency for self denial which means your child will prefer to bottle up feelings and emotions rather than talk over problems with you. This is why it is important to be able to communicate, and to continue to encourage him or her to mix with other young people.

One factor to remember is that your child needs to feel useful from an early age, and wants you to be proud that you have a Capricorn in the family. The way you bring up your child is going to have a great influence on the future years, because more than many other signs, a Capricorn searches for perfection and security.

It is highly unusual for Capricorns to neglect their parents, and your relationship could become even better with the passing years.

Growing up

AQUARIUS

Growing up can be a marvellous experience for an Aquarian. There is so much to see and discover in the world, and school days will provide a whole host of new experiences.

A touch of extra discipline could be necessary, for even though your child may be a genius with mathematical equations or scientific experiments, he or she may not accept more mundane requirements. It is important to point out that even Aquarians have to adapt to some extent to the ways of the world.

Naturally not every Aquarian child is going to become a

genius, nor turn into an Aquarian rebel, but the onus of finding the right balance in your child's life is going to be your responsibility and it may not always be easy. If you insist on forcing your will and opinions on an idealistic child you could easily be branded a bore and a non-thinker, and might even turn your child away from you. You should, however, realize that throughout life, your Aquarian may be slightly more unconventional than people born under some of the other signs, and it might be as well to try and make a few allowances for this.

You can help your child by explaining both sides of any issues. Aquarians tend to need causes to believe in, but must be able to distinguish between true and false humanitarianism. Your child should be encouraged to join clubs and societies where he or she can meet young people with the same interests.

Perhaps this is the moment to point out that your child should be disciplined into training his or her mind to concentrate. Although I frequently read that Aquarians are absent-minded, I wonder whether it is simply that as children they were so busy observing and making mental notes of what was going on around them, they neglected many things they had been asked to do. It is up to you to point out that a good memory is a positive characteristic.

It would be wrong to try to change a positive thinker into a negative one. It is naturally a question of balance and being accepted as a trusted friend and not simply a dogmatic parent.

Adolescence can be a time when some of the rebellious qualities of Aquarius emerge. It is a phase when the Aquarian desire to act and appear different from everyone else could also lead your child along wrong paths. Don't be too hard on your son or daughter if you find their clothes outlandish, but do keep as careful an eye as possible on their activities outside the home. Try to point out that some good healthy exercise probably wouldn't go amiss, for some Aquarians can be very lazy, although others might display their unpredictable characteristics by becoming runners or racing drivers. It seems almost natural that James Dean, being an Aquarian, made films (such as "Rebel Without A Cause") which fitted in with so many of the Aquarian characteristics.

You must remember that your child should learn that all experiences are not positive, and that it is important to be able to decide what experiences are not worth having.

With loving guidance, your child should be able to step from adolescence into adulthood with a great deal of confidence.

Growing up
PISCES

Now that your baby is growing up into an impressionable youngster, more guidance may be needed. Even allowing for his or her highly intuitive qualities, a Piscean child can easily be drawn into the wrong company. Remember that Pisces is considered one of the most unselfish and self-sacrificing signs of the Zodiac, and your child will always have faith in people. Piscean children are sometimes unmercifully teased or bullied by their more extrovert companions who feel that shyness is something unworthy, so try to make your child understand that self-defence may sometimes be necessary and that running away from problems will not solve them.

If you feel your child's shyness or moments of quiet withdrawal could create problems when starting school, why not speak to the teachers about this. Naturally not every Piscean is going to grow into an introspective teenager, but two things are certain; understanding and praise are vitally important to Pisceans of every age. You may discover that your child has a creative streak which should obviously be encouraged, and whether the talent is for art, music, dancing or acting, you may have a very gifted youngster on your hands.

Something else you may have already had to accept as one of the inevitable factors of growing up with a Piscean is that your home may become a refuge for all the homeless animals in the neighbourhood, as well as human lame dogs your child may encounter in the course of a day. Compassion is a positive quality, especially these days, so do not be annoyed, but point out as gently as possible that your home may simply not be large enough to cope with all this.

It is probably the right moment to point out that Pisceans are often the most impractical people in the entire Zodiac when it comes to dealing with money. Try to train your child at the earliest possible age to learn not only its value but also how to spend it wisely or you will have continual demands for extra pocket money. Be sure that your child doesn't turn into yet another Pisces adult who doesn't have the faintest idea of how to budget from one week to the next.

Sport may not be a favourite occupation of your Piscean child, and if it is, it's probably because of a Sagittarian ascendant or some other planetary aspects in the natal horoscope. However, whilst plenty of sleep and moments of quiet are always important to this sensitive sign, it is also important that your child doesn't grow up into a lazy adult who hates the thought of any kind of activity and tends to fall asleep in a stuffy room.

Pisceans are sometimes unfairly accused of being weak, gullible individuals, but you will soon discover that although your child may find it difficult to make decisions, he or she certainly possesses a determined mind. This is where your understanding of the inner needs of your child is highly important, for a Piscean who grows up discontented or disillusioned with what life has to offer can simply drift along without any goal.

Try and erase any threads of self-doubt and insecurity which intrude into the mind of a Piscean. The capacity for great success is sometimes hidden away in an apprehensive soul, so your encouragement can be a powerful force in leading your child towards a happy and contented adult life.

FINDING YOURSELF

... *the 18–25 phase*

Growing up is one stage, and the lessons you have learned along the way should have helped prepare you for the future. However, perhaps you were sometimes protected too much by your parents, school teachers or even your friends. Suddenly there is a whole new world to conquer, and perhaps you are a shy Piscean who becomes insecure when confronted by new people or new situations, or maybe you are a hard-working Capricorn who is determined that school days were only the beginning and that you are now prepared to scale the highest mountain in your search for success.

The way you tackle your life from now on is immensely important, and obviously you are going to make some mistakes, for no one is one hundred per cent perfect, not even a self-critical Virgoan. However, if you know from the start that because you are a headstrong Arien you are likely to fall headlong into love without using any judgement, perhaps you won't make quite so *many* mistakes.

The stage has already been set, and you have already learned some of your lines. You can't crawl back into your cradle, or run home crying because a teacher has scolded you for obtaining bad marks in an examination paper. You have to learn to fend for yourself now, which makes this one of the most important phases in your life because it will certainly influence your later years.

It's the time when you will have to decide how you want to earn your living, when you will begin to plan your lifestyle, and decide whether you are the settling down type who needs security, or if there is some Sagittarian wanderlust inside you. It's also the time when you become more concerned about your health and fitness; it's your responsibility to look after yourself now. Generally your very first love affair hits you in a big way too. Sometimes it lasts a lifetime, sometimes only a few weeks, but almost always it leaves a deep impression. Maybe you never realized that the impression it does leave can also depend on your star sign, and there will be an opportunity in this part of the book for you to read about the signs with whom you are supposed to get along best.

When I started writing this book, I decided to ask all the people I knew if they could remember their very first love affairs. Almost all of them could, but the ways in which they remembered them were very different, the most romantic description of all coming from a Piscean, true to form.

The 18–25 phase is especially important because it is often the time when big decisions need to be made. It was once the vogue for girls to get engaged and married early, but times have changed. Many women in this age bracket today have successful careers, and their domestic life sometimes has to fit in with their work. Men don't usually have the same problems, but for them it is certainly a time when the right choice of career is highly important.

During these years, you probably feel you can afford to be idealistic about life, but it would be wise to remember that your idealism should be combined with down-to-earth reality. Knowing more about your sun sign personality doesn't mean you can walk through life sheltered from all the problems facing everyone else, but at least it should give you a head start in knowing how to deal with them if they do arise.

The 18–25 phase

ARIES

Your emotional life....

If you're a typical Aries you may fall in love a hundred times before you decide to settle down. Perhaps this is an exaggeration, but admit it, when you meet someone new don't you sometimes feel "this is really it, at last", and after a few weeks, or months, don't you also sometimes yearn for a new challenge, a little more excitement, the thrill of a new romance?

This is a period when your idealism can be a problem, because you want to believe in a "happy ever after" existence, and unless you are learning to be more rational and realistic, it could also be a period when some of your dreams could turn into disasters, and when your Aries energy and vitality might be channelled in the wrong direction. It is, therefore, an immensely important time.

I am certainly not telling you not to fall in love, for that would be completely alien to your nature. Besides, it is usually good for you to have someone with whom to share your interests, who understands you, and with whom you can plan for the future and have a happy family life. If, therefore, all this sounds appealing to you, why must you so often try to turn an exciting love affair into something it perhaps can never be, because the personality of your partner does not blend with your own?

In Astrology there are four elements – Fire, Earth, Air and Water. You already know you are a Fire sign, and you certainly have many fiery qualities, but fire can be tamed, and perhaps you do sometimes need a little taming. Otherwise you may continue to run rampant through life, falling headlong into unsuitable relationships and situations. One of your excuses may be that you hate to be given advice,

75

because you feel it is best to learn by your own mistakes, but how many times do you want to repeat the same errors? Considering how much you hate boredom and repetition it is amazing how many Ariens follow a pattern of one unsuitable relationship after another. You have gone through childhood and adolescence and falling in love can be wonderful, but perhaps love for you should be something which grows a little slower, in order for it to be lasting.

Astrologers say that your ideal lovers and friends should be the other Fire signs, Leo and Sagittarius. However, as an Aries, I have often found that most of the people closest to me are Librans, plus a few Taureans, Virgoans and Cancerians! Other people you should get on with will probably include Geminians and Aquarians.

Your working life ... and earning a living

Maybe school bored you, and you decided university was a grind leading to nowhere because of all the unemployment in the world, but no one should ever underestimate your intelligence or your desire to be successful.

Because your ruler is Mars, the God of War, astrology books say that Ariens should be soldiers, explorers, pioneers, and surgeons, but what is certain is that you need an outlet where your own particular talents and abilities can be developed. Advertising, Public Relations, Journalism, Broadcasting and Television may especially appeal.

Don't expect to take command of everything in the first week of a new job. It's about time you realized that although Aries relates to the first house of the Zodiac, pertaining to the ego, you simply cannot continue to use your "me first" attitude on the rest of the world. As long as your efforts are appreciated, and you feel stimulated in what you are doing and with the knowledge that your prospects are promising you should be happy.

If you start off on the right track now you should be able to organize your financial situation. Ariens tend to have an ability to keep the money flowing in, but it can sometimes flow out again too easily! Impulsive spending may be normal for you but if you don't keep it in check now, by the time you reach twenty-five your financial situation could be gloomy. You are usually extremely generous to the people you care for, which can sometimes present problems if your income hasn't reached a level where you can honestly afford this.

The idea of saving whilst you are young may seem distasteful to you, but it would be worthwhile talking to a friendly bank manager who could advise you on a personal saving scheme which will give you some security for the future.

Obviously, it is impossible to give you specific advice about a career without looking at your personal horoscope, but here are some general "dos and don'ts".

POSITIVE	NEGATIVE
Always look for a challenge.	Don't expect to conquer the world overnight.
Make sure you feel really enthusiastic over your choice of job.	Try to be more disciplined.
	Don't continually change jobs.
Try to be self-employed, free-lance, or work with people you respect and like.	Don't give up on tasks half way through.
Aim for an executive position.	Make sure you aren't carried away by an exciting sounding job and forget to enquire about the salary.
	Never take a dead-end job.

LIFE-STYLE

The right life-style for an Aries is sometimes difficult to pinpoint, but tends to go hand in hand with the right emotional life, the right job, and the right social environment. It is impossible to generalize and say that you need to be in the heart of a busy city. Many Ariens do thrive in this type of atmosphere, but you may be equally happy in rural surroundings, provided the bright lights of a city are not too far away.

Perhaps you should avoid settling down before you've seen something more of the world. The old maxim "marry in haste, repent at leisure" might well have been written for Aries. You could save yourself from resentment later on by making a list now of all the things you want to do in life, and trying to achieve most of them before you reach the settling down stage.

Your life-style may be centred around an active existence, and having acccepted that your insistence on rushing around and your refusal to relax can make you accident prone, you should be calmer by now. Exercise is usually good for you because it helps to burn up your excess energy, but you should also make sure that you allow yourself enough hours of sleep at night. If you do insist on being overly active you can be prone to headaches. It is also wise to have regular dental check-ups, as many Ariens tend to suffer with teeth problems.

The way you handle your life now is of utmost importance. People are always saying it is never too late to change habits, and maybe that can be true, but if you resolve to set yourself a pattern which would make major changes unnecessary, then surely it will make the future much easier too.

The 18–25 phase
TAURUS

Your emotional life

Taureans tend by nature to be sensual, loving but also possessive. Venus, Goddess of Love, certainly seems to have influenced you in your desire for creature comforts, and by the time you reach eighteen, with your practical and realistic instincts well developed, you usually know what you expect from your emotional life. You are determined not to make any of the mistakes you have seen other people make, for a Taurean love has not only to be for real, but also for keeps.

This is a time when you should take a long hard look at what the world has to offer you, and at what you are prepared to offer in exchange. You don't want to take the important step of settling down with the first person you have a relationship with, unless you are sure that you could spend the rest of your life with him or her.

Remember that it can take you a long time to get over emotional upsets, and you can even become instilled with a sense of distrust if someone really lets you down, so this is definitely a time to learn about the type of partner who would be right for you. Without knowing your personal horoscope, one can only make generalizations, and Astrologers tend to pick the other Earth signs of Virgo and Capricorn as ideal partners for you, although I can think of at least two stormy but successful relationships between Taureans and their opposite sign of Scorpio. You may also find yourself sharing some of the same sentiments and need for security as a Cancerian.

Once you do fall in love, usually nobody can influence your decision. You are probably conducting your emotional life in your slow, sure and careful way, but don't stifle your emotions and keep your feet too firmly on the ground Remember you *are* a sensual person, and not only a picture of common sense and practicality. Don't settle for a relationship simply for the sake of security, because a fulfilling emotional involvement is highly important to you.

You are probably happier when you know friendship is developing into love. You don't realize how lucky you are, for many people don't have the patience to do that, but planning the right emotional set-up during these important years will benefit you enormously in the future.

Your working life and earning a living

You may have worked your way conscientiously through school, may even have decided that university was going to be profitable for you, and that now is the time to set your mark upon the world. You are often perfectly happy to take a minor position to start with, as long as you feel financially secure. Taurus relates to the second house of the Zodiac, which is connected with possessions and personal security, and a regular income is a necessity for you. Work on a commission basis would only start you worrying. However, if you have creative abilities, try to find a job which gives you a chance to express them otherwise you will only become frustrated later on in life. Venus endowed you with an eye for art, colour and design and an ear for music, and whilst your Taurean appreciation and understanding of money tends to mean that you should make wonderful bank managers, accountants, property dealers, economists, and estate agents, you may just as easily be drawn to farming, architecture, and the world of the arts.

Be positive about what you do want to achieve, and don't spend your life following in someone else's footsteps. Never give anyone the chance to accuse you of being one of those plodding Taureans sitting at the same desk for years without promotion. Aim just a little higher and make the right use of your self-control, practicality and common-sense, whilst admitting that you enjoy earning your living and watching your bank balance grow.

You're unlikely to be wildly extravagant, even at this age. At times you can almost be too self-controlled, so once you start earning a good living, don't give the impression that you resent spending money on enjoying yourself. You certainly shouldn't have to worry too much because you are one of the signs least likely to become bankrupt.

The following guide will give you some general "dos and don'ts" on what to look for when choosing a career,

80

although it is of course impossible to be specific without knowing your personal birth chart.

POSITIVE

Look for a position where your capable and practical qualities will be appreciated.

Choose an established organization with congenial workmates.

Aim for security but don't hide away any creative talents.

Always spend sufficient time looking for a job which you feel suits your personality, because you have to remember that you dislike making changes very often.

NEGATIVE

Never undervalue your talents.

Don't always put financial gain before an exceptionally interesting job opportunity, unless of course it is necessary.

Don't ever be too hesitant about taking an executive position simply because you are accustomed to following other people's orders.

Don't be stubborn about accepting constructive advice or tackling tasks with a new approach.

LIFE-STYLE

The life-style for a Taurean is not usually too difficult to predict. Many of you tend to associate a domestic life with the surroundings you grew up in yourself. If your family have always had to be careful about money, you will probably feel that once you earn your own living, you should provide as much comfort as possible for everyone in your family. Bricks and mortar are important to Taurus. If creature comforts appealed to you from an early age, it is wise to remember that you would probably be very unhappy leading a nomadic existence. Remember you are a Fixed Earth sign, you are fixed in your feelings, your ideas, your personality and you will probably want a fixed life-style.

If you work away from home before you marry, make sure you always stay at the best possible place you can afford. Don't begrudge paying the extra money this could cost you, because if you can afford it the importance of feeling comfortable cannot be over-estimated.

Deep at heart you're often a nature loving person. A

crowded city may be acceptable, especially if you have a good home with your favourite possessions around you, but you often feel the need for trees and greenery.

Try to spend the years between eighteen and twenty-five wisely, which doesn't mean ignoring a happy social life whilst busily planning for a secure future. Taureans sometimes become lazy, which can lead to overweight, so always ensure that you look after your body and eat the correct foods.

Taureans dislike adapting to change, and if you don't plan your life carefully now it is unlikely you will feel like altering it later. Do make sure you can achieve the security you desire, but don't forget to allow your sense of humour and creative abilities to develop as well. You don't have to be a stick-in-the-mud just because you are an Earth sign.

The 18–25 phase

GEMINI

Your emotional life

Perhaps being classed as a flirt when you're eighteen doesn't worry you unduly, but surely you don't want to go through life changing partners continually do you?

One of the negative aspects about your restlessness and need for constant change and variety, is that you may lose the perfect partner. It's rare to find all the desirable qualities in one particular person, and your problem is that often the qualities you desire seem to change as often as the weather.

On the positive side, you generally don't waste too long with someone who is completely wrong for you. Love at first sight, based only on physical attraction isn't likely to last if there isn't also a strong mental communication.

Astrologers tend to link you with the other Air signs of Libra and Aquarius. The personality of your opposite sign of Sagittarius, might also blend with yours, for you both often seem to need to feel inwardly free.

The 18–25 phase can be extremely important. For many, it could be when you do settle down, even if it is with someone who perhaps in later years turns out not to be the soul-mate you had yearned for. It's definitely a learning phase, and if there is one activity you are exceptionally good at, it's learning and absorbing, taking in everything which comes your way, evaluating it, and then probably eliminating the things you no longer consider valid for your particular life.

It's a time when you should be starting to make your way in the world, and in many ways if you are a typical Gemini you might be better off not tying yourself down to the demands of a steady relationship, although that of course depends on your own particular horoscope. Some Gemini butterflies need to spread their wings and flutter a while before alighting in any one spot for long. If that sounds contradictory to some of the earlier paragraphs, I say it because I have known too many Geminians who went into early marriages before they had sown their wild oats, and who became jaded and depressed when the marriages went sour.

Try to use this phase in your life as one when you make lots of friends, enjoy an interesting social life, move around as much as you can, and don't tie yourself down just because all your friends are doing so. They may not be Geminians and have your characteristics. Try to let your mind and not your heart rule your emotions, even though it may seem tough, and if a permanent relationship is of paramount importance always make sure it is with someone with whom you can communicate on every possible level.

Your working life and earning a living

If you are being talked into a dead-end situation in your very first job, whoever is trying to persuade you should definitely have more sense, as routine is often your idea of hell.

Remember Mercury, the messenger of the Gods, who is your planetary ruler? You definitely need to communicate, so obviously something connected with the world of the media could be ideal for you. The fields of journalism, publishing, television, politics, teaching and salesmanship can all be enhanced by your presence. If none of these appeal, or have an opening available, you will have to think again, but do think hard because this is an important phase, and it is only a stepping stone in your working life. When you start off in the right field your attention will not wander and you will put in every possible effort in your determination to succeed.

A Gemini should always be able to emerge financially stable even though the economic situation is not particularly encouraging these days. However, bright and imaginative as you are, you do tend to be impractical with money. You seem to have inherited a happy-go-lucky streak from your opposite sign of Sagittarius, for there are some of the characteristics of our opposite sign in all of us, but even so it is no use going through life assuming that everything will be fine just because you want it to be. Make sure you don't acquire a reputation for forgetting to repay debts. It's not that you mean to forget, it's usually just that you tend to have so many other things on your mind. Why not learn to calculate your weekly expenses and eliminate unnecessary extras, for this will be a useful practice all your life.

This guide will help you with some "dos and don'ts" on what to look for when choosing a career.

POSITIVE	NEGATIVE
Make the most of your ability to communicate both verbally and in writing.	Never take a routine job.
If you are good at languages try to find a job where you are able to use them.	Don't take a position where you have to "clock in" unless you make a firm resolution always to be punctual.

84

Look for variety in your work and a place where you can not only meet interesting people but also have a chance to travel.

Make positive use of your inherent "sales technique".

You have a bright and imaginative mind — so use it constructively.

Don't lose interest in something before you've spent enough time evaluating your future prospects.

Don't take a job where you are left on your own too much.

LIFE-STYLE

Your life-style, especially during this phase of your life, can sometimes be erratic. You are not usually keen to make a firm commitment regarding house buying because you probably haven't decided where you really want to live. It's that Gemini restlessness and search for the undefinable which makes you hesitate about putting down roots. Enjoy your freedom, provided you are doing what you really want to.

If you're a typical Gemini, who loves a change of scene as often as possible, and travel opportunities come your way, then take them. You were probably exceptionally quick at picking up languages whilst at school, and you might even decide that living and working abroad for a period is just what is needed to broaden your mind. That's what life is often all about for a Gemini, mind-broadening. Remember, though that you're an adult now, and can't go through life shirking responsibilities and jumping from one situation to another without a backward glance. It's all down to concentration again, and to your hunt for the elusive. Never forget that by searching too hard and too far afield you may miss the objective that was close by you all the time.

You need lots of mental stimulation in your life, and there should be no need for you to feel lonely. You have an innate gift for starting up conversations, and because you usually have interesting contributions to make, it's unlikely that you would ever be accused of being a bore, but you can be exhausting, and conversations with you can be very one-sided!

Don't forget that all your nervous energy needs a release of some sort. Don't set yourself a pattern of staying up late because you could become an insomniac. If you want to keep your youthful Gemini looks, then you must give yourself plenty of fresh air and exercise, and relaxation too.

The 18–25 phase

CANCER

Your emotional life

By the time you have reached the age of eighteen, your childhood dreams of romance may have turned into reality at least once. You may not necessarily be as romantic as a dreamy-eyed Piscean, but you are certainly a good runner-up in the emotional stakes.

It is necessary, however, to retain a sense of balance. Romance for you shouldn't simply be walks in the moonlight, holding hands and tenderly kissing your lover, whilst dreaming about a happy ever after future. If you are a typical Cancerian romance needs to go hand in hand with security. Your own family background will probably influence you a great deal. Remember how impressionable you have always been, and how important it is for you to feel secure? Even if your first romance was one of those head-over-heels affairs more befitting an impulsive Arien, you are bound to decide that a comfortable and stable domestic life is what you yearn for deep inside your heart.

This stage of your life is also especially important because any emotional knocks you receive now might put you off falling in love again for a long time. You might start to bury your deepest emotions under your mythical shell, which would be wrong. Nearly everybody suffers upsets at one stage or another, and if you are really honest with yourself, perhaps you will realize that some of the problems

86

could be your own fault for being too idealistic and unrealistic.

Remember that because your birth sign rules the fourth
house of the Zodiac, which relates to home and family, you
probably won't be truly happy unless you choose a partner
who shares your feelings about domestic bliss and understands your personality. Wanderlust tendencies and extravagant spending in a partner are unlikely to tempt you even
whilst young. Someone as sentimental as you are would seem
an obvious choice and you might relate especially well to
a Piscean, another Water sign, although his or her financial
impracticality could worry you too much. Scorpio, the third
Water sign is also supposed to be ideal but you may find
some Scorpions too intense and passionate. Capricorn, your
opposite sign, shares your need for material security but
perhaps is not emotional enough, and a great deal will therefore depend on your own particular horoscope.

The desire for a happy home and a family to look after
can sometimes make you too clinging and possessive. Don't
spoil your chances of a successful emotional life by tying
an invisible cord around a partner's wrist. Remember that
caring deeply for someone doesn't mean that you must try
to possess him or her.

You usually have a sense of humour, but learn to develop
it, because often when someone says or does something
which you feel is directed against you it is almost as if a
cloud comes over your face to hide the hurt you feel. It
may, however, simply be your own sensitivity which over-
reacts and means that you have misinterpreted the situation.

Cancer, although you are ruled by the Moon, do try to
keep your lunar moods bright and optimistic, and stop
giving way to melancholy thoughts. Stop worrying about
rejection, and learn to sparkle just a little more.

Your working life and earning a living

There is one word that often describes you perfectly – dependable. One of the reasons for this is again that inherent desire

for security. A steady job which pays a reasonable salary is often one of the first things you think about once you leave school or university.

However, never forget that you are a leader. Because you are a Cardinal sign you are full of enterprising qualities, and even though you may be content to sit back and take orders whilst learning your trade, it probably won't be too long before your marvellous memory and ability to adapt to your environment will enable you to make considerable progress.

Ideally you are suited to work which gives you the chance to make use of your financial abilities. You could become a brilliant economist, or be very successful in the hotel business, or in buying and selling property. Dealing in antiques would appeal to your love of history, and you would make a good teacher, nurse or social worker. If you have strong creative abilities, don't be hesitant about using them, because it is terrible to feel frustrated in your working life, and nothing would be worse for your colleagues than having to put up with a sulky Cancerian.

Your financial situation will usually be fairly secure as extravagance is not often in your nature. Once you start work you are bound to make a realistic budget for yourself and stick to it. You understand the value of money and hate to see it wasted, especially if it has taken hard work to earn it.

The following guide gives you some "dos and don'ts" on what to look for when choosing your first job.

POSITIVE	NEGATIVE
Make sure you choose something where your capacity for hard work and sense of responsibility is recognized and appreciated.	Don't allow your moods or depressions to interfere with your working life.
If looking after people comes naturally to you, find a job where you can make use of this quality.	Don't work in an office on your own if you are someone who needs to have people around.
	Don't suppress your talents and abilities simply because you

Ensure that your salary is sufficient to provide the domestic comforts you require. are tempted by something boring which pays more, unless there is a major reason for your choice.

LIFE-STYLE

Life-style for you is often fairly unadventurous, as you may be quite content to stay with your family until you feel the moment is right to strike out on your own. This doesn't necessarily mean that you are afraid to be more independent but that you are content to be amongst the people with whom you grew up, and also enjoy contributing to the household expenses now that you are earning a living.

However, if your home life wasn't happy, don't be afraid to make your own niche in the world. Remember that people can sometimes feel lonelier in a crowd than when physically on their own. When you do find a place of your own, remember that your creature comforts are important to you, and that you will need a kitchen large enough to indulge your love of cooking. Whether you choose a busy city environment or a small town or country village, you should soon be able to create a homely atmosphere.

Try not to be a Cancer woman who plays the "mother hen" to everyone you meet. I remember one client who was desperately in love with a successful business man, but she fussed over him so much that one day he turned around and shouted that he already had one mother and didn't need another. Happily they both had a sense of humour and knew enough about astrology to realize that the maternal instinct is an integral part of your sign, but allowing it to take over your personality could influence your life-style in a negative way.

Don't view everyone you meet as a prospective marriage partner because you should also realize that life can be fun when you are single.

Make sure you always take sufficient exercise, and look after your digestive system and stomach. You sometimes have a bad habit of making yourself ill through giving way to negative thoughts and worrying too much, and this could lead to ulcers. However, if you take care of your body, your health shouldn't give you too many reasons to worry, and as physical discomfort is unbearable to most Cancerians, you are usually determined to stay fit.

The 18–25 phase

LEO

Your emotional life

By the time you have reached the age of eighteen, you may easily have fallen in love about half a dozen times, or at least you thought it was love. Suddenly you meet someone who seems to be a perfect partner, and you turn a deaf ear to advice from parents, friends or colleagues. You are convinced this is really it. Perhaps the partner you have chosen isn't completely convinced, but with your own particular brand of love and affection, combined with your Leo forcefulness, you intend to overcome that little problem, and make your love story one with a happy ending.

However, don't you realize you can land yourself with many problems if you have to talk someone around to your way of thinking? Do you really want to be the dominant partner in a relationship? Because if not, you'd better think twice before you get yourself involved in situations you might regret later.

When it is time for love and romance, it would be wonderful if you could let your partner take the leading role some of the time. Perhaps it's not so bad for Leo men, but a Leo woman can create problems for herself by being such a forceful personality, sometimes attracting weaker partners who end up resenting and trying to destroy the very strength which first attracted them.

You are ruled by the Sun, and you love to make people happy. When you are in love, nothing gives you greater pleasure than to feel loved in return, but it is certainly not being positive if you give the impression of demanding that love, so use your strength to advantage, let the people you care for know that you can always be relied upon, but that you will never try to hold on to them too demandingly or organize their lives without being asked.

Aries and Sagittarius tend to be the obvious choices of astrologers as ideal lovers and companions for you, because they are also Fire signs. The attraction of opposites means an Aquarian may fascinate you, but you could find the unconventionality of this sign a little hard to take, whilst a relationship with another Leo might certainly prove to be a challenge.

This phase of your life should be marvellous. You love to have a busy time socially, and it should be easy for you to make lots of friends and have a great deal of fun. It's not necessary for you to settle down too early. A happy home life is important to you, but you're not usually as security conscious as a Taurean or as domesticated as a Cancerian.

Your working life and earning a living

If you were asked early on in life whether fame or fortune appealed to you most, as a Leo you would tend to answer "fame".

Even if you have not decided what you want to do, by the time you have left school, you know one thing, you want to be a success.

It's simply not in your nature to sit back and take orders from other people for the rest of your life, unless those orders are given by someone you respect, and who will, in turn, respect you. Needless to say, you are better as an employer than as an employee, but you can't expect to achieve that position overnight, unless your own particular horoscope happens to show a great deal of good fortune as well as other beneficial aspects.

If there is something you have set your heart on, which might mean a few years of extra study, try to do it. You are not afraid of hard work, so the results should be worthwhile. You are also unlikely to give up half-way. You may need encouragement from other people, but that shouldn't be difficult to find. If you decide to go into management training, you could certainly become an excellent manager, and if ever someone was a natural for the world of show business in one form or another, it's you. However, that is probably generalizing too much about a profession in which there are obviously insufficient opportunities for every aspiring actor or film director. You could become a good teacher, although sometimes you may be just a little too fixed in your opinions and unforgiving when mistakes are made. The world of fashion would appeal to your creative and artistic talents, and as an organizer you are usually excellent.

Once you start to earn your living you would be well advised to try and control the extravagant streak, which tends to be part of the Leo personality, before it gets serious. This especially applies if you are doing a study or training course and have very little spare money to spend. You often like luxury just a bit too much, and learning to plan and stick to a reasonable budget once you start work is often essential for you. Even if you do feel that fame is more important than fortune, you subconsciously seem to expect the fortune to be there too. You enjoy being an expansive host, but first make sure you are solvent enough to pay for the party!

Put your will power and determination to really positive use, and aim to be financially successful, for it will tend to make your life much easier, especially as when buying clothes you so often aim straight for the designer labels!

The following are some general "dos and don'ts" on choosing a career, without of course being able to take into account your own personal horoscope:

POSITIVE

Aim for something which gives you the chance to demonstrate your powers of leadership.

Make sure you will have a chance to express your creative talents.

Ensure you are in a position where your knowledge can help other people.

Try to find an atmosphere where your extrovert personality will be appreciated and where you will also make new friends.

NEGATIVE

Don't expect to take control on your first day at work and start bossing everyone around.

Don't allow your pride to become a negative characteristic by refusing to take orders or accept constructive advice.

Don't ever take a job which gives you very little opportunity to achieve the kind of success you desire.

Don't try to impress colleagues by extravagantly flinging your first week's salary around even if you do want to be generous.

LIFE-STYLE

It's not difficult to visualize the ideal life-style for you. Your surroundings must always seem like a castle to you. You want to be proud of the way you live. However, you are not usually very tidy, and perhaps you should organize yourself a little better.

If you have a home of your own now, but in the past had parents who spoiled you unnecessarily, you will have to guard against being lazy. For an energetic Fire sign, you sometimes slip far too easily into inactive moods and must discipline yourself more.

You are often happier living in a busy town where there is plenty of activity, for you are one of the most sociable of all the signs. You love to entertain, to go to theatres and cinemas, and enjoy life in as many ways as possible. If, because of love or circumstance, you have committed yourself to living in the heart of the country, make sure you are not going to be too isolated, for you do enjoy having people to talk to, and the chance to shine in your own particular environment.

In this phase of your life, there may be some dreams you haven't yet fulfilled. Perhaps they relate to a career ambition, perhaps to seeing more of the world, perhaps simply to discovering more about yourself. Enjoy what is around you, but remember not to be too self-assertive. Remember too that your Leo pride which can be so positive could also turn into a negative quality if you are never willing to accept that even you can sometimes make mistakes.

The 18–25 phase

VIRGO

Your emotional life

The perfect love affair may be something you have dreamed of and read about during your most impressionable years. Once you reach eighteen or nineteen, you may think you know exactly what you are looking for, but it may be difficult to find someone who measures up to your ideals.

This can be a problem for Virgo, because in the same way that you would hate to feel second best, you would find it hard to accept as a partner someone who didn't reach your high standards. Your friends may accuse you of being cold and calculating but it is unlikely they will have many reasons to call you promiscuous. This is not to say you are necessarily passionless, but love for you is something you hope will be for keeps, and until you do surrender your Virgo heart, you are probably quite content to enjoy a busy social life and have plenty of good friends with whom to spend your time.

Romance for you may develop slowly from a platonic friendship, which can be a good way to have time to sum up every aspect of someone's personality and to decide whether it is really going to blend with yours.

However, you may fool a lot of people, but it's silly to

fool yourself. You are often as romantic as the rest of us underneath and, when you fall in love, you may turn from a cool and somewhat detached Virgoan into a passionate person whose Sun sign seems much more likely to be ruled by Fire.

Try to accept romance as something which can be wonderful but may have its difficult moments too. If it goes wrong, realize that there must have been a valid reason for it, and for heaven's sake don't start to survey the next person you are attracted to with an even more critical eye.

You may have a fantastic memory but don't always insist on trying to recapture the romantic past because you could be disappointed.

Settling down and getting married early isn't necessarily a typical Virgo trait, especially if you have decided it is more important to study for a chosen profession. You are also more capable and self-sufficient than some of the other signs, which often means you are perfectly happy to live on your own for a while, or at least until your idea of true love comes along. At this stage of your life you sometimes prefer physically unemotional friendships which enable you to keep your mind clear.

There is definitely one thing you should have learnt whilst growing up, which is that being analytical may be fine at times, but if you apply too much to relationships they might come to a speedy end, so if you don't want to lose out on the chance of a happy future with a loving partner, don't insist on perfectionism every minute of the day.

Being overly critical can be negative, but on the positive side you are usually prepared to go to the ends of the world to be with someone you love.

However, don't start to worry if you reach the age of twenty-four and haven't yet met your ideal partner. Try occasionally to imitate your opposite sign of Pisces and survey the world through a mythical pair of rose coloured spectacles, because you can have a great deal more fun that way.

Perhaps only the two other Earth signs of Taurus and Capricorn would live up to your high ideals, but if you could learn to criticize people a little less you might discover that you get on extremely well with some of the other signs. Pisces might be a good match, because of the attraction of opposites, but an especially dreamy and impractical Piscean would irritate you. Mental communication should be good with Gemini.

Your working life and earning a living

Having read that you are known as "the sign of service", you should realize that there must be many worthwhile opportunities for you once you start work. You could be marvellous in publishing, accounting, nursing, anything to do with health and hygiene, book-keeping or secretarial work, and you probably could be an ideal theatre critic. Routine doesn't bother you, in fact you may put in longer hours sitting at your desk going over details than almost any other sign.

However, don't be like one Virgo friend of mine who has been in the same job for twenty years without being especially happy or fulfilled, but who has felt too insecure to risk searching for something more interesting. If you have a special talent, perhaps all you need is someone to encourage you to use it. Besides criticizing other people, you sometimes give yourself a hard time too, and can be unbelievably shy about pushing yourself forward. I don't think, though, that I could advise you to take a gamble over earning a living unless I knew your personal birthchart. The need to earn a salary which enables you to save a little is important to you and in itself is a positive trait. You do not usually waste money, so try not to worry about your outgoings, for generally you have the ability to work successfully and earn a good living.

Don't decide that you are going to sit on the same chair at the same desk for year after year unless you are totally convinced that it is what you want to do. Besides, while not necessarily admitting it, even to yourself, you do usually like recognition, perhaps not in the same way as an Aries or Leo, for you may not necessarily aspire to be a leader or in the public eye, but you do want to be appreciated for your conscientious and efficient work.

The following guide gives some general "dos and don'ts" on choosing a career.

POSITIVE

Choose something where your critical and analytical approach to projects will be a positive attribute.

Remember you may be happiest in the kind of work which gives a service to the public.

If you always worry about financial security, choose a career where the long-term prospects seem sound.

Make sure you do something which gives you the opportunity to use your mind well, as you tend to be highly intelligent.

NEGATIVE

Don't undervalue your own particular talents and be too self-critical.

Don't aim to find absolute perfection in your working surroundings because it may not exist.

Don't let your desire to serve mean that you put in long hours being highly efficient at a job which doesn't pay you commensurately with your efforts.

Don't go into any kind of career or business which seems risky as you would probably spend most of your time worrying about it.

LIFE-STYLE

Unless you have many planetary aspects affecting your personality, with your exact time of birth giving you an Ascendant totally in contrast to your Virgo character, your life style is going to be described by two particular words – "neat" and "tidy". Whether you live at home, at university, have a place of your own, or marry early, your surroundings will reflect your orderly personality and the way you probably intend to continue. This would be a good moment to repeat, however, that not everyone can be such a paragon as you, and a few things out of place don't mean the end of the world. Besides, I know a Virgo woman who lives blissfully happily in a rambling old farmhouse where tidyness is practically an impossibility. It all depends on your priorities, and sometimes yours are just too pernickety. If you plan to live with someone who is by nature untidy, of course it may be difficult, but look upon it as a challenge, or better still learn to compromise.

You are over the usual childhood illnesses now, and unless there is medical evidence to the contrary, you should be basically a healthy person. Look after your body properly, but don't be one of those Virgoans who becomes known as a hypochondriac and fill your medicine cabinet with every known pill and ointment for ailments you may never get.

Hopefully you won't have had a family who gave in too much to your fussy attitude over food, for that can be something which irritates other people and also spoils your own enjoyment of life. Besides, you can even become a gourmet cook if you are able to forget about analysing each and every ingredient contained in the recipes you choose.

The 18–25 phase

LIBRA

Your emotional life

Librans may not be as blatantly sexy as some people born under the sign of Scorpio, but they rarely fail to attract admirers. By the time you reach eighteen you are probably revelling in your popularity, and one of your only problems might easily be whom to choose as a date for Saturday night.

Your sign relates to the seventh house of the Zodiac, which in turn relates to partnerships, and marriage, and at this stage of your life, an ideal partnership is something you would probably like to find. Although you are unlikely to rush headlong into unsuitable relationships like your opposite sign of Aries, you can sometimes make mistakes by taking so long to decide about someone that finally he or she retreats.

Settling down too young could also be a mistake, because your desire for a partner with whom to share your life might make you oblivious to some of the negative characteristics of the person you choose, those which may not blend especially well with your own. There usually needs to be a strong mental communication as well as a physical one for you, and although you are not necessarily fickle, you would not be very happy to be involved with someone who looked askance at the mildest of flirtations.

Emotionally, you may not like to be alone for too long, and that is something you should perhaps try to overcome so that you don't make the wrong choice of partner.

Because you are both idealistic and sentimental, you might hate to think of a future with no one to share it with. However, it would be ridiculous to think that way, because if you are a typical Libran, your basic personality and characteristics are such that people will invariably enjoy spending time with you.

As an Air sign, you are continually seeking mental stimulation and new ideas, which also means that you need a partner you can look up to and respect. Your first romance may sweep you off your feet, and you may be bowled over by passionate declarations of love, but if there isn't something deeper underneath, it may not last.

I can think of at least three Librans who did marry their childhood sweethearts, but somehow they outgrew the partners they chose, and a restless Libran usually refuses to stay restless for too long. For all your soft and gentle ways, there is often a strong self-protective streak below the surface of your nature, which usually prevents you from living with mistakes forever.

As an ideal lover, friend or colleague, perhaps you find

that fiery Aries adds something to your life because of the attraction of opposites. However, Gemini and Aquarius are the two signs generally linked by Astrologers with your own since like you they belong to the Air element. As your planetary ruler, Venus, also rules Taurus, you might perhaps find romantic bliss with a Taurean.

Your working life and earning a living

Vague and indecisive you may sometimes still be, but at least you should be aware by now that because you enjoy wearing beautiful clothes and having beautiful things around you, it is vital for you to earn a living.

You usually need to work with other people. Even if you build up a business entirely on your own, there should be at least one person whom you can trust and relate to. It doesn't matter if it is a secretary, an adviser, an accountant – just as long as it is someone who can help you see things in their right perspective should your Libran scales start to tilt again.

Librans can become excellent artists and poets, beauty specialists, hairdressers, diplomats, air stewards and stewardesses, and personnel managers, and are often marvellous working in public relations or in the world of fashion and entertainment industry. Your sense of values, your urge for justice, and desire for harmony could also lead you to a successful career as a lawyer. Your main problems may only stem from deciding in the first instance exactly what you do want to do.

However, by now you should certainly know what you are good at, and, depending on your own personal horoscope, it might well be something I have not mentioned. Don't feel insecure about taking your first step into the working world, and make sure you don't get talked into accepting a job which you know is wrong for you simply because someone you care for expects you to do it.

If you have set your heart on taking up an occupation which needs further study, and the financial situation is difficult at home, perhaps you can take a part-time job to help.

Your career may have to last a long time, because even if you do settle down and start a family whilst still very young, it may not necessarily be easy to find a partner to provide for it and your extravagant tastes too.

Obviously it is impossible to be completely specific without looking at a personal birthchart, but here are some general "dos and don'ts" to look for, when you choose your career:

POSITIVE

Look for something where you can be part of a team.

If you have artistic or any other creative abilities, make full use of them.

Try to find something which enables you to use your natural charm, tact and diplomacy, and where your environment could also lead to an improved social life.

Always remember that for you to give of your best, you need surroundings which are harmonious.

NEGATIVE

Resolve to put away your indecisive, vague and lazy characteristics.

Don't aim to work completely on your own unless you are sure you will feel happy.

Don't take on something where you feel you would be caught up in union disagreements, because you could spend so much time trying to settle arguments that your work would suffer.

LIFE-STYLE

Although you may dislike to be alone too often, you probably equally dislike the idea of spending your life in a noisy crowded environment where your deep need for tranquillity is impossible to satisfy. However, it might be inadvisable at this stage of your life to bury yourself in the heart of the country, with only a herd of cows for company.

You may prefer to stay with your immediate family until you meet the right partner, or to share a place with a friend with similar interests and with whom you can relax.

If circumstances do force you to live in a busy town, see

that your home surroundings are as comfortable as possible, for it is impossible to over-estimate the importance of comfort to your sign. Your good taste should enable you to furnish a place without being extravagant.

Enjoy the life-style you choose, and don't start asking yourself if perhaps you should have done things differently, for by now you should have learnt that hesitation and self-doubt can be very negative characteristics.

Remember to take care of your body properly, especially as excesses of food and drink can sometimes lead to problems with your kidneys. I know several Librans who find Yoga particularly helpful as it gives them an inner area of peace after a hectic and crowded day. If you balance your days with the sufficient amount of rest and exercise, you should be able to stave off illnesses. Always remember that this kind of balance is especially important for Librans.

The 18–25 phase

SCORPIO

Your emotional life

By now you have learnt enough to realize that being known as the "sex symbol" of the Zodiac doesn't have to imply that your emotional life should consist of a series of amorous adventures reducing you in later years to a tired and somewhat jaded Scorpio man or woman.

However, at this stage in your life, and depending on the other signs, planets and aspects affecting your own personal chart, you are often concerned with finding the right balance for your personal life. You may be involved with your first real romance, or determined to pass important exams, or excited at the prospect of a marvellous career, but that right balance is important because otherwise you can become far too intense and drained.

One of the first things you have to learn about love is to try to practise your self control a little harder and never allow strong feelings to turn into brooding and destructive jealousy. You have a great deal to give, but it's time you recognized your own faults. Admit it – you hate anyone to be jealous or possessive about you, yet if the person you are involved with can't account for almost every moment of his or her day, you can be hurtful and destructive.

Perhaps one of your troubles is that although you may be reasonably uninhibited when it comes to sex, you are inwardly searching for a perfect love relationship, but sometimes you are so suspicious that you could ruin your chances of achieving happiness.

Make a decision now to enjoy romantic involvements in a much more positive way. If you hate to be possessed, try to understand your partner's feelings. Let the relationship take it's own time to develop rather than allowing your Scorpio power and intensity to frighten away someone who might be perfect for you. St. Francis De Sales once wrote "Nothing is so strong as gentleness; nothing so gentle as real strength". Make sure there is gentleness in your emotional life, Scorpio, because you certainly have the strength.

Because of the intensity of your emotions, it could sometimes be difficult for a cool and detached partner to understand you, and perhaps the other two Water signs of Cancer and Pisces would relate best to you. Your opposite sign of Taurus can be as sensual and possessive as you, so at least you should have a great deal in common as lovers.

Your working life and earning a living

If you are a typical Scorpio, a good salary is an essential part of the job you choose, because you do enjoy spending money. Invincible Scorpio, you usually strive courageously to reach the heights of your career. Your shrewd mind and intuition often help you to be in the right place at the right time, and to make the right contacts.

Perhaps the ideal job for a Scorpio would be a private detective, or even writer of mystery novels. You may be drawn to religion – Billy Graham is Scorpio. Astrology books tend to list you as "surgeons, undertakers, butchers, scientists, psychiatrists, lawyers, reporters, spiritual healers and psychic investigators", but the truth is that once you set your heart on achieving a certain goal, then no one is likely to deter you. Jobs which offer little scope for your own particular talents usually soon make you resentful and stubborn, and if you thought that Taurus was the only stubborn sign in the Zodiac, ask a colleague how it feels to work alongside a Scorpio who is bored and fed up.

You are a loyal employee, provided you are never slighted, or your loyalty doubted in any way. If that happens, perhaps it would be best for you to think seriously about leaving that particular job, because the atmosphere would never be the same again. Also, don't start flaunting your sex appeal amongst your fellow workers. Your career is one thing, and your emotional life should be separate.

One of the wonderful assets of being a Scorpio, is that with your strongly burning desire to climb to the top, you are not afraid of hard work or setbacks along the way. However, remember that making a martyr of yourself can be negative and lead to exhaustion. To suggest again that perhaps you could be a little less intense will probably make you laugh, but at least have some enjoyment and don't become a slave to your work.

Obviously, without looking at your personal horoscope it is impossible to be specific on choosing a career, but here are some general "dos and don'ts" for you to keep in mind:

POSITIVE	NEGATIVE
Make use of your talent for research and investigation.	Don't give the wrong impression of yourself at a

Trust your intuition, if a job opportunity sounds right for you – it probably will be.

Remember that if you really want to achieve a goal, your strength and determination will help you.

If money represents power to you, make sure you take a job with good financial prospects.

first interview by "coming over too strong".

Don't expect to have a position of power in your first job.

Don't search for a working environment simply as a place to find new admirers.

LIFE-STYLE

Life-style for you depends on what you have achieved so far. However, whether you are still living at home, are sharing with a friend, or have settled down with a partner, you will certainly demand one small area which is completely yours, and where no one can intrude without your permission. This may annoy a few people, but all it means is that you always desperately need some privacy, and if you recognize this need it should help you respect the feelings of other people you might hurt.

At this stage, many Scorpions enjoy having a place on their own, a "bachelor pad" where they can conduct their life in their own way before settling down. It may simply be that you are not prepared to share yourself completely with a partner before you have discovered more about your own personality. You enjoy your freedom, reading late into the night, or watching crime or horror films on television without interference.

You are also at the age when an exciting night life may be beckoning you, and providing you don't allow this to interfere too much with your work or your financial situation, it shouldn't do you too much harm, but moderation should be your keyword.

You are often more shrewd than many other signs, and if you have not reached the age where you want to settle down to get married and raise a family, then don't. However, you should always remember that there is more to

105

a relationship than physical communication alone, and with your good mind you need people around you who can at least match you in intellectual exercise. You will also need a partner with an inner strength you can respect, for someone who is weak will tend to bring out your own negative qualities.

You will still enjoy indulging your love of sports, but hopefully you have toned down your desire for speed and danger. Exercise is good for you, but don't wear yourself out with excesses Scorpio, for even *you* need some moments of relaxation to give your inner soul a little peace and harmony.

Because Scorpio relates to the eighth house of the Zodiac, which in turn relates to death, legacies, regeneration in the spiritual sense, self-sacrifice and joint finances, you sometimes tend to take life so seriously and with such self-control that your inner power shines through and makes other people a little wary about becoming involved with you. Perhaps to be really positive you should sometimes be less secretive over your feelings, and even learn to laugh at yourself a little more.

The 18–25 phase

SAGITTARIUS

Your emotional life

Once you have reached eighteen, you have probably already mentally vowed to retain your independence. Naturally this doesn't mean that the idea of falling in love and settling down is something which fails to arouse your interest. On the contrary, you enjoy romance, especially when you have someone who obviously thinks you are wonderful.

However, your need to feel inwardly free without having someone trying to possess your every thought is extremely important. At this stage in your life you often prefer to keep relationships on a light-hearted level, and a jealous partner giving you the third degree over where you were last night could almost put you off marriage for life.

You had better be careful, though, Sagittarius, because your desire for freedom and love of adventure may lead you into too many flirtations and give you too casual an approach to sex. Often for all the wrong reasons you start thinking of marriage as a life sentence, whereas by looking around you at some of your happily married friends, you should see that it needn't be any such thing.

The phrase "lucky in love" could almost have been invented for you. Your ability to find admirers who are attracted by your frank and open smile, your enthusiasm, vitality and ability to feel and look at home in almost any surroundings, should be considered a blessing.

The strange part is that sometimes you handle romance in such an awkward manner that you antagonize the very people who were first attracted by your personality. Don't be such a know-all, don't try to take command on your second or third date. Just think how you would react if the same treatment was handed out to you.

Sometimes you fool yourself and say that you are more interested in having lots of good friends than in falling in love and settling down with just one person. I've heard it said many times by Sagittarians, and I've yet to meet one who isn't starry-eyed and bursting with happiness when they feel they have met their ideal partner.

Don't set your sights so high that it is impossible for anyone to measure up to them, and make sure you find a partner who can stand up to you or later on you will be bored.

If you want to spend your adult freedom without being serious about any one particular person, of course that's your own choice. Just don't be so determined to feel free that you let the perfect partner slip by, for he or she may not come round again.

Friend, lover, husband, wife – above all you need someone who won't make you feel as if an invisible chain is round your neck. Your opposite sign of Gemini should understand this, but although you are supposed to get on exceptionally well with the other Fire signs of Aries and Leo, they may, at times, seem too demanding for you. Libra and Aquarius should at least share your love of company, but not necessarily your desire for an active life.

Your working life and earning a living

The urge to spread your Sagittarian wings and fly could easily apply to your working life. Something which gives you the opportunity to travel and expand your horizons will be very appealing, now that it is time to earn a living.

If the family budget will allow it, you may have decided to go to university and study for a degree. You often make excellent philosophers, lawyers, social administrators, teachers, sports promoters and sportsmen, politicians, interpreters, and writers, whilst your ability to express yourself also leads many Sagittarians to search for fame and fortune in the entertainment industry. Your ruling planet Jupiter once again endows you with a certain amount of luck, and you often have the ability to fall into the perfect job simply because you are in the right place at the right time. However, you should definitely not allow yourself to become overly optimistic and think you are going to achieve instant success in your chosen field simply because you are a Sagittarian.

No one should doubt your intelligence, but sometimes you lack direction and can drift, simply because you feel your luck *is* going to change. Perhaps it will, but you should never assume that this will happen. Be aware of what you are getting involved with when you do take your first job as too much routine or desk work can be disastrous for you. Ideally, you'd make a perfect explorer or big game hunter, but there is not room for many of those! You are usually at your best when you feel you can be your own boss, because you resent too much supervision, but as it is unlikely that you will achieve this in your first job, it would be wise to learn to accept orders with a little more grace.

Starting work means the opportunity to earn your own living, and as it may also coincide with having a home of your own, you obviously need to consider the question of salary carefully. It could be all too easy for you to jump at the chance of an apparently exciting job, which might not bring you in sufficient money to support you in your desired style. Perhaps this may not be so important for a practical Virgo or Capricorn who nearly always manages to balance his budget, but if saving has never been one of your virtues, it is something you will probably need to learn about. Don't be afraid to ask your bank manager for some advice. It may seem like another door closing on the freedom you yearn for, but it is necessary.

It is impossible to be specific on exactly what to aim for when choosing a career, without looking at your own personal birthchart, but here are some general "dos and don'ts":

POSITIVE

If you love an outdoor life and lots of travel, try to find something which offers this.

If you hear of something fantastic, but feel you'd never stand a chance go for an interview anyway, as with your luck, anything can happen!

To be free-lance or self-employed may seem less of a threat to your freedom than a regular 9–5 job.

NEGATIVE

Don't involve yourself in a partnership or business without taking professional advice first, for sometimes your optimistic quality can be misplaced, and you often fail to examine everything carefully.

Never take a job without knowing exactly how much you are going to earn each week. Working on commission could be wrong for you because of your inclination to over-estimate.

Make sure you never walk into an interview thinking you know more than the person interviewing you, or try to conduct an interview the way you feel it should be run.

LIFE-STYLE

Your happy-go-lucky personality will be much in evidence by now. Living at home with the rest of your family probably doesn't appeal nearly as much as having a place of your own before you settle down. It isn't necessarily that you want to get up to all sorts of wild and exciting antics, but simply that you do need your independence.

Your sign has sometimes even been referred to as the "bachelor" sign, because many Sagittarians do prefer to stay single for longer than many other signs. However, if you happen to be a Sagittarian who hates the idea of living on your own, then you will probably be equally happy sharing a place with a friend.

It isn't just a joke when you read that Sagittarians tend to live with a suitcase packed ready to take off on a trip. You often do travel more than many other people, because you welcome every opportunity to do so. Therefore until you have decided how you want to organize your life, it is often better for you to rent a home than tie yourself up with a mortgage. However, always remember that you usually do love the open air, and that even if you don't indulge in energetic sports, you certainly need some exercise for your active mind and body. You would soon feel hemmed in by a tiny living space, or with no green fields within miles; and whilst I wouldn't dream of expecting you to be as neat and tidy as Virgo – it wouldn't hurt you to learn to be just a little more organized now that you are no longer a child.

The 18–25 phase

CAPRICORN

Your emotional life

If you are a typical Capricorn you are not likely to rush headlong into wildly unsuitable love affairs without thinking first. You tend not to want emotional dramas in your life, but usually desire a solid conventional relationship which brings you security.

However, with life ahead of you Capricorn, you can be just as romantic and passionate as people born under other signs, except that you are inclined to discipline your feelings to such an extent that your image is cool and aloof.

Saturn's influence gives you this serious and self-disciplined attitude to life, but provided you use it in a positive way, it can only be constructive. Should you develop into an inhibited pessimist and a prude, you are certainly missing the whole point of this book. Everything in life is a question of balance, and as you may have spent your childhood years being more serious than the rest of your friends, perhaps this should be the time when you start to unwind and enjoy what life has to offer you. I am certainly not suggesting that you should suddenly become promiscuous or treat romance too casually, but try to be less cautious about every admirer who comes your way.

Perhaps more than any other sign, financial stability influences your choice of a partner, and it would be very difficult for you to lower your own particular standard of living, no matter how desperately you were in love. However, beware of becoming a social climber.

I remember a Capricorn client who when young married a man whose personality in many ways blended perfectly with hers. However, I could see in her chart that if there should be any financial problems in the marriage it would go through a very difficult time. Unfortunately, her husband ended up bankrupt and a few years later the marriage was on the rocks. It is not that the woman was particularly mercenary or materialistic, but her Capricorn personality simply couldn't cope with the thought of living precariously in the future; and to be fair she had warned him many times that he needed professional advice over his affairs and he simply didn't listen. If he had, it might have turned out differently, because Capricorns can be extremely loyal and do everything possible to help a loved one.

You are often more sensitive and insecure than other people realize, and need a partner who not only understands this, but who teaches you to relax a little more. Don't deny yourself the chance of romance during this phase just because you are being overly practical about life. No one is asking you to live in a garret on love alone, but learn to release your fears and be more optimistic or you could lose the perfect partner.

A partnership with one of the other Earth Signs, Taurus and Virgo, is supposed to suit you best, whilst your opposite sign of Cancer will often share many of your material ideals. It is hard to generalize for you, as so much can depend on your own particular horoscope and on whether you are a Capricorn who always prefers to let your head rule your heart, or whether you are also a romantic.

Your working life and earning a living

You really do fit the symbol of the goat surefootedly circum-navigating the rocks and crevasses and finally reaching the mountain peak. It could be said that Capricorn is the sign of the business man or woman, and although that may be generalizing too much, it is true that you are often the hardest working and most ambitious of all the signs.

Capricorn rules the tenth house in the Zodiac, which in turn relates to one's status in the world and to one's career. Material success is your criteria in life, and you seem to have an ability to ignore any impediment which might prevent you from achieving your goals. Perhaps this is also one reason why you are often so exacting in your choice of partner, because the world, for you, is a serious place, and you don't want to make any mistakes. You would hate to be dependent on other people when you are older, and it is essential for you to work towards financial in-dependence.

If your chosen career demands study once you have left

school you will do it willingly. The business world is a natural place for you, but whatever you choose you will apply yourself to it conscientiously, seriously and responsibly. Capricorns are supposed to make ideal scientists, teachers, farmers, builders, politicians, bankers, civil servants, administrators and organizers of all kinds. On the more lighthearted side, I can think of one who was virtually a professional gambler, had a series of financial setbacks and then became a highly successful business man; so whatever you do, it is likely that you could end up on the winning side. Your sign often has a highly creative streak, with a love of classical music.

Your need for recognition usually means you will not take orders from other people once the chance arrives to prove your own worth. You don't mind how long it takes just as long as you achieve your objectives in the end, and this naturally involves earning enough money to keep you and those closest to you in the manner fitting to a Capricorn. This doesn't imply extravagance, but simply means that everything you buy must last, whether it's a house, a car, or clothes, and you are well aware that quality can cost a great deal.

Always remember that by nature you are an ambitious person, and when you step out into the working world make sure you choose employment which gives you the potential to fulfil your ambitions or you might become bitter and dissatisfied in later years.

Here are some general "dos and don'ts" to remember when choosing a career, although without looking at someone's personal birthchart it is obviously impossible to be specific:

POSITIVE	NEGATIVE
Because you are so ambitious and hard-working always choose a job which offers you excellent prospects.	Try not to expect colleagues to live up to your own high standards and to be as ambitious as you.

Always make positive use of your organizing and administrative abilities.

Remember you often prefer to be left to work on your own where no one can bother you.

The business world is usually ideal for you.

If the financial situation is extremely important, choose something which pays overtime, as staying late will never bother you.

Don't hide away creative talents just because you feel that real money can only be made in the business world.

Make sure you don't accept a position simply because you think you will become an executive in the future, without taking into account your happiness in the years in between.

LIFE-STYLE

Until you can afford to live in a manner which fits your requirements, you may be happier to stay with your family. "Steady" is the word which would best describe both you and your life-style. You can't bear to live in a disorganized way, and even if you only have one room it is bound to reflect your personality. You are often as neat and tidy as a Virgoan, and are usually prepared to cut down on any non-essential items in order to save money for the future.

You are usually much happier with a mortgage than paying rent. You like to see a return for your money, and even if you won't actually own your property for about twenty-five years you feel more secure. Don't stint yourself too much on comfort, because with your tendency towards hard work, you do need to be able to relax and enjoy some leisure moments.

If you have settled down with a partner at this stage, it is important for you to live in the right surroundings. You will be very particular in your choice no matter where you reside, whether town or country, and you often prefer to know who your neighbours are before making a final decision.

You are also determined that when the time comes to raise a family you will provide every possible comfort, and perhaps this desire is one of the reasons other people sometimes unfairly criticize you for being so materialistic. You don't necessarily want money for what it can bring you personally, but in order to make life easier for others. You often have something of your opposite sign of Cancer inside your personality, the desire to make a nest for your family.

Capricorn, as you drive yourself harder than many of us, it is important to remember that your body is not a machine. Relaxing may seem like laziness, but it is necessary, and with your tendency to suffer from sensitive skin, you can succumb to rashes or allergies all too easily if your body is not looked after. You don't have to imitate the mountain goat, but some good brisk walks in the fresh air could make you feel alive again after an especially heavy day, and meditation could help calm your over-worked mind.

The 18–25 phase

AQUARIUS

Your emotional life

Your reluctance to settle down in a permanent relationship at this stage of your life is often linked with a need to be free to pursue your own ambitions without feeling responsible for anyone else.

Although not necessarily the most passionate of people, you are a dreamer and idealist, and it would be untrue to say that you do not need a partner to complement your life. The problem could be that with your personality, someone who tried to tie you down either mentally or physically could soon encounter your defiant side. It is not that you prefer to indulge in casual love affairs rather than be involved seriously with one person, but finding the right person can be difficult and you might prefer to surround yourself with friends and acquaintances who appeal to your mind rather than to your heart.

Hopefully your parents understood your personality sufficiently when you were younger and impressed upon you that if you want love and affection, you must be less impersonal in your manner.

Have you never realized that dogmatic or tactless remarks when directed at someone who is attracted to you can be destructive? Aquarians can break a great many hearts without even knowing it, so at this stage of your life try to make a determined effort to understand the feelings of other people a little more.

If you have already met someone with whom you can communicate on all levels, perhaps he or she should read up some of the characteristics of Aquarius. It is not that you are going to be unfaithful, but you don't want to give up your friends, your ideals and your causes even when you do settle down. Make sure you don't expect to have things all your own way and then become angry if some of your partner's interests don't necessarily include you.

Perhaps you should always seek out another Aquarian for love and marriage, because the two of you would either have a great deal in common or nothing at all!

Above all in a partner, friend or lover, you need someone who is prepared to understand your temperament and doesn't expect effusive declarations of the way you feel. Virgo and Capricorn should therefore suit you in some ways, but you could find it difficult to sustain a relationship for long, and might discover you get on best with the other Air signs, Gemini or Libra. An involvement with your opposite sign of Leo could at times be stimulating, but you might find you spend too much time trying to dominate each other.

Aquarius, you who are so concerned with humanity as a whole, can sometimes make such unnecessary mistakes in your own emotional life by being too detached. With life ahead of you, see that you start off on the right path. You have a great advantage over many of us, because your flashes of intuition can often help you more than advice ever could.

Your working life and earning a living

Being such a progressive thinker, you may well have decided to go to university, but once you start to search for work, one of the most important factors for you to remember is that it would be most unwise to consider a routine job as you would probably soon become bored.

Careers which make full use of your creative and imaginative abilities are ideal for you. The influence of Uranus draws you to radio, television and the cinema. You could be a scientist, and would be invaluable to NASA. You are certainly an ideas person, but sometimes need help with your schemes. You would be marvellous looking after people and animals, whilst your attraction for causes will often draw you into politics, where you could however become too unorthodox in your tactics.

Don't allow your desire for independence and free speech to make you a person who dictates to employers or workmates just because you feel your ideas are the right ones. They may well be, but you need more tact and diplomacy if you want to make a success of your working life. Also, at the risk of being repetitive, I must point out that dressing unconventionally is all very well in the right surroundings, but if you insist on going to work in an office looking like someone from the Russian Steppes you have no one to blame but yourself if you are subject to raised eyebrows.

With your original and imaginative approach, you are likely to achieve success in whatever career you choose. However, as you invariably have a free and easy attitude towards money, it is important not to take a job just because it appeals to you intellectually, for remember you have to live on the salary it pays.

It is impossible to be specific about how to choose a

career, without looking at a personal horoscope, but here are some general "do's and don'ts":

POSITIVE	NEGATIVE
Find something where your imagination and flair for the unusual are used in a constructive way.	Don't be so obviously way-out in your ideas that you create a bad impression, especially at a first interview.
You are an ideas person – you need projects in which to throw yourself whole-heartedly.	Never ever take a routine or dead-end job.
Think about working on your own as you are usually happier giving orders than taking them.	Learn to understand that a new way of doing things isn't always the best, and be more prepared to listen to constructive advice or you will become unpopular.
You need constant stimulation, change and variety in your work.	
You always need to retain your own individuality even in a large organization.	

LIFE-STYLE

How could any astrologer be expected to generalize on the life-style of an Aquarian when you are noted for your reluctance to follow any set pattern?

It is often no use your family expecting you to lead a neat and orderly existence. You honestly don't care too much about your surroundings as long as you are comfortable. However, when you have your own place, you tend to be drawn to modern furnishings, stainless steel and futuristic paintings.

Aquarius relates to the eleventh house in the Zodiac, which in turn relates to "one's hopes and wishes", group activity and friendships which don't tie one down. Whether you are single or settled down by now, you may find yourself happier in a town than buried in the heart of the country, as you do need a variety of people around you. It would be a good idea to join a club, preferably where sport is involved, because exercise could become very necessary at this stage if you have realized that you are becoming lazy.

This phase of your life can be one of the happiest, because you often feel sufficiently independent to do all the things you longed to when reading about them as a child. You may also enjoy travelling and meeting people from other countries.

Do remember, however, that your desire for a free and easy life-style can make you very difficult to live with, and if you are embarking on a serious partnership, make sure that your ideas are compatible.

The 18–25 phase

PISCES

Your emotional life

If you could turn your adolescent dreams into realities, many of them might include a fairy tale romance in which you and your chosen partner would live happily ever after. However, Pisces, by now you should have realized fairy tales are one thing and the modern world is real and earnest and rather different.

A perfect emotional life is of great importance to you. You must be careful, however, that the idea of romance doesn't blind you to the faults of the person to whom you choose to give your heart. You choose the most unsuitable people especially when you are young, placing them on some imaginary pedestal and being shattered and distraught when you realize the whole situation is simply an illusion. Of course this isn't going to happen to all of you, but it is a trap which needs to be carefully avoided if you are going to live a really positive life.

Falling in love can also make you neglect virtually every other area of your life, including your health and your finances, but just remember that you are getting too old to go running to your parents with tears in your eyes. Learn to control your emotions now, because when you do find the right partner whose personality blends with your own, you can have a very fulfilling life. Perhaps a Piscean truly needs a more forceful sign to cope with those vague and vacillating ways, but if you fall in love with someone for their strength and practicality, make sure there is plenty of romance in their character too, or it could lead to unhappiness.

Ideally the signs supposed to be most suited as partners for you are Cancer and Scorpio, as they fall under your own element of Water. Although opposites often attract, a relationship with a Virgo could leave you deflated because of the criticism you received. Librans could often satisfy your need for romance, but might be too indecisive and easy-going.

You are generally prepared to overlook convention, and financial security, as the idea of renouncing all for love sounds so romantic to you, but do rely more on the intuition which was bequeathed to you at birth. It is your innermost psychic awareness which will tell you whether you have found a perfect partner, or whether you should enjoy this stage of your life without feeling it is imperative to settle down.

Your working life and earning a living

There are so many careers you could choose and you could do well in all of them, once you have made up your mind that the real world can offer you more security than a dream one ever could. Not that you are necessarily searching for material security, but you must realize that for someone as disorganized about practical issues as you, it is highly important. Astrology books tend to list you as writers, actors, poets, musicians, psychics, nurses, teachers, social workers, sailors and priests. You're not always very business minded, although again this is a generalization, but few people would deny your creative and imaginative qualities.

In some ways you are a person who wants success without putting in the necessary efforts to achieve it. You have a deep need for recognition, and whilst you will work very hard for a job or cause that you believe in, should you feel discontented or unappreciated, you become unexpectedly stubborn.

A Pisces who believes wholeheartedly in what he or she is doing is positively inspired, and will enjoy every moment of the working day. This is why it is so important for you to examine your own needs carefully when you have to think about your first job. If you decide to continue studying after finishing school, it could well be the arts which attract you, and hopefully you will have enough people around to encourage you to exploit your talents and not start to have second thoughts about them.

Although you could enjoy working for large companies, you would soon sink into your own private little world if you felt yourself misunderstood in any way, because of your sensitivity to atmosphere and surroundings. If you are your own boss you will certainly have to try to be more organized and disciplined.

It is impossible to be specific about everything to look for when choosing a career, as obviously this will also depend on your personal horoscope, but here are some general "dos and don'ts":

POSITIVE	NEGATIVE
Helping people less fortunate than yourself often comes naturally to you, so look for a worthwhile opportunity to make use of this ability.	Don't drift through life taking whatever comes along because it seems easier that way.
You are often at your best in an artistic field, once you forget about your shyness.	Don't let your inability to balance budgets mean that you take a job without knowing you will be able to cope on the salary it pays.

You are very susceptible to atmosphere, so the right working surroundings are important to you.

Don't lose yourself in your dream world and expect opportunities to be presented to you without having to do the groundwork yourself.

Never give the impression that because you are dreamy, you cannot take responsibility when it is necessary.

LIFE-STYLE

At this stage of your life, a great deal will depend on whether you are romantically involved with someone with whom you want to set up home, or whether you are content to stay with your family. You are not particularly adventurous or independent, and therefore the idea of having a place of your own may not necessarily appeal, but if you do decide to share a flat or house with a friend, make sure it is with someone whose way of life is not going to conflict with yours. You have always liked your creature comforts and sometimes have a bad habit of finding yourself with high mortgages or exorbitant rents simply because you fall in love with a romantic atmosphere without considering your financial situation.

Be careful that with your sympathetic nature you don't find yourself providing a home for your less fortunate friends. Whether you decide to live in a town or a city, peaceful surroundings are most important for you. Pisceans often are happiest near water, but wherever you choose try to find a place where you can afford to indulge yourself with your daydreams for just a few minutes of your day.

One of the weaknesses of your birth sign is a tendency to enjoy social drinking, so take care that it never becomes an alcoholic problem. Do get the right amount of sleep and try to banish worries from your mind before you go to bed, otherwise your nights will be restless and you will wake up feeling tired.

Pisces, you may be an expert at calming other people,

and helping them with their problems, and perhaps some of you even possess a healing quality too. This doesn't mean, however, that you are an expert at running your own life. You must remember that a life-style full of pressures is bound to create difficulties for a sensitive and gentle soul such as yourself. In Astrology, Pisces relates to the twelfth house of the Zodiac, which in turn relates to "the secrets one keeps hidden from the rest of the world and to one's own undoing". In order to be really positive, you should realize that although looking after other people is worthwhile, it shouldn't mean that you have no time to look after yourself. You are not a child any longer, so take yourself in hand and become more practical from now on.

THE CHANGING TIME

... the 25–35 phase

This is the time when Saturn, the so-called Task Master of the Zodiac, influences you into taking a long hard look at yourself, and teaches you a few more of life's lessons, which could range from taking on greater responsibilities to re-organizing your life pattern.

Between the ages of twenty-five and thirty-five, many of you will have settled down to a family life, or if you decided that a successful career is more important, you may be doing extremely well by now. Are there times though when you feel that maybe something is missing? Have you achieved everything you thought you wanted, only to realize with horror there is still something lacking in your life? Don't worry, it is perfectly normal, and not happening to you alone.

I believe that one major astrological influence in our lives is the planet Saturn, who in mythology was personified by the Romans as Saturnus, God of Agriculture, founder of civilization and social order. He was also identified with Cronus, the Greek God of Time. Today astrologers often refer to him as "The Task Master of the Zodiac". Certainly Saturn's influence tends to make us work hard for what we want out of life, but also brings the rewards in return.

"So what," you may be saying, "how does that affect my life, especially now?" Well, some planets move faster than others, the Moon changes signs roughly every two and a half days, but Saturn takes approximately twenty nine and a half years to traverse the great wheel of the Zodiac and return to the place it occupied when you were born; and in case all this sounds horribly complicated, there is a table at the end of the book to show you when Saturn was and will be in each sign.

When Saturn returns to its original place in your natal horoscope, it invariably coincides with an important time in your life. Obviously this will affect everyone in a different way, because it will depend on your personal horoscope, however an influence will be felt.

My own feeling is that Saturn really does bring us all to task, and that when the planet reaches the period around our twenty-ninth year, we are almost compelled to re-evaluate everything in our lives, and if necessary prepare ourselves for some reorganization.

In many ways, it is as if an individual's true path in life is not totally formed before the first Saturn cycle has come to pass.

If, therefore, you are around twenty-nine years old and are inwardly feeling that one part of your life is coming to an end, without being able to understand why, subconsciously you could be picking up the stirrings of Saturn's transit in your horoscope, perhaps bringing to light any difficulties or limitations you may be facing.

Saturn's influence teaches patience, willpower, and above all reality. It makes you think objectively about clearing the dead wood out of your life, and it should help to pave the way to a more positive future.

I feel it is important to repeat that the exact area of your life which is going to be most affected by this Saturn cycle depends on your own natal horoscope, but you will probably sense a need for change yourself. It isn't something which is necessarily going to happen overnight, for Saturn can take up to two and a half years to pass through a sign, but always remember that this should be a constructive phase and one that in later years you will look back on as a turning point to a happier and more satisfying life.

The 25–35 phase

ARIES

Your emotional life and life-style are usually blended together now, but if you still have not learned to take life at a slightly slower pace, the years between twenty-five and thirty-five can be tricky for you. Some of you may have already been through a first marriage, and sometimes a first divorce. Your job changes may have been too numerous to even think about, and your headstrong ways may still be irritating your family, friends and colleagues.

Suddenly you seem to feel more restless than ever, you can't bear the thought of your life rushing away from you. Has it begun to seem like a vacuum? Do you suddenly feel trapped in an existence which is becoming more and more alien? Does excitement only seem near when you go to the cinema or read in the gossip columns about other people's lives?

Perhaps you've suffered the first major loss in your life, a loving parent or favourite aunt? Someone who was really important to you in the formative years of childhood. This is no real reason to throw everything away and become homeless, jobless, or desperate for a new romance. It simply means that you may have finally realized it is time to grow up. Now you really do have to stop approaching life as if you were charging into battle on your fastest steed.

When Saturn returns to the place it occupied in your natural horoscope at birth, when you are around twenty-nine and a half years old, you may at times feel as if a burden has been placed upon your shoulders, and that setbacks and limitations seem to come about for no apparent reasons. However, if you look on the positive side, you can surely see that slowing down and re-evaluating your life can be highly beneficial, and enable you to be much happier in the future. Now you should be wiser, able to take stock of past and present situations in a way you never were before. At last you can prove to other people that the Arien qualities of leadership are not lacking in you, and that they are going to be applied to every area of your life in a constructive way. It's almost as if you are being given a second chance to recognize and correct your bad points, and so strengthen your vulnerable areas.

The knowledge of the kind of life-style you really do want should bring you greater happiness and stability once you have accepted the importance of being a wiser and less impatient Aries. Your dreams and idealism don't have to disappear, but your talents and abilities should be channelled in the right direction.

Accept this period as a turning point in your life, and use it to its best possible advantage. Sometimes this can mean hurting other people, which isn't easy for you. However, there is probably no way you can hide what you are going through. You also hate making mistakes, and it may not be easy to admit that perhaps the marriage you rushed into at twenty two has changed now that you have reached your thirties.

I remember an Arien actor friend of mine, who once fell desperately in love with his leading lady in a television play, even breaking off an existing relationship to enjoy a whirlwind courtship and marriage, sadly to realize not too long after that neither of them was really right for the other. Now that same man is happily married to someone else whose personality blends perfectly with his, and they have an adorable baby son. Saturn's influence helped him towards a greater understanding of the demands love can make.

If you haven't learnt to curb some of your energetic ways, this may start to show physically, for vitality is one thing but you can't expect to keep up with the eighteen-year-olds all the time.

This doesn't mean you have to give up all thoughts of an exciting, active life; exercise is good for you. It just means a little more care may be needed. You may be working harder than ever, with a family to look after, and lots of domestic chores, so do try to allow yourself some time to relax. You will see the benefit of it, even if it only rests your active mind. Perhaps you could take up meditation.

Your working life

If you married whilst very young, and gave up work, perhaps you are now starting to feel the urge to start again, even to try out an unfulfilled talent, and it may well be beneficial for you to supplement your life with a new interest now. You are certainly unlikely to complain about being over-worked if you are completely absorbed in the events of your day.

This is also a time when some Ariens may decide to switch careers, even successful ones they have built up from scratch, to go into a completely new field. You will probably discover if you ask around that many people who made major job changes in their lives after they reached twenty-eight went on to become even more successful. In many ways, your goals are now more certain in your mind. You don't want to spend the rest of your life switching jobs every few years unless it becomes inevitable. You are no longer quite so carried away by daydreams, for you have a long way to go yet, and you are prepared to work hard to get there.

The 25–35 phase

TAURUS

It's often when you are approaching thirty that you start to have doubts about your life. You may have planned everything carefully, and haven't had to, or wanted to make many changes, but your subconscious values are now changing.

Perhaps you have been so determined to make the right marriage, to safeguard yourself financially, to live in a certain area, that you have forgotten all about that little Taurus child who liked to smile and play happily. You've become so caught up in the rat race and in preserving your creature comforts, that you feel bogged down in routine. However, when Saturn goes back to the place it occupied at your birth, you are given a chance for self-analysis, and if you dislike what you see, there is an opportunity to do something constructive about it.

Therefore if you have reached this stage, and are searching for a way to a more fulfilling life, you should realize that if you are prepared to recognize and tackle problems, there can still be a great deal of happiness ahead. Don't be one of those stubborn, obstinate Taureans who refuses to face facts. If you are putting everything you possibly can into your life, and are getting absolutely nothing out of it, don't you think you owe yourself the opportunity to change?

This happened to a Taurean client of mine who reached a crisis point in her marriage around the time of this Saturn cycle. It made her realize that her need for security wasn't great enough to compensate for her financially stable but emotionally rocky marriage, for she had chosen a partner whose personality seemed totally incompatible with her own. Having to make changes was not easy for her, but she realized that letting a negative situation drift on was bad for everyone involved. Needless to say the story ended happily for both people are now married to more suitable partners.

A crisis in your life often does come with the first Saturn cycle, but obviously it will be different for everyone, depending on your own personal horoscope. Saturn's influence tends to make you evaluate your past and decide, if necessary, to re-construct your life. A need for security is probably still paramount, but now you should start to realise that security can come from inside yourself. Once you accept this, you begin to feel free and find the "real you".

In many ways your life-style could also have become more settled now that you have reached this phase of your life, and hopefully you are counteracting any tendencies to be lazy or over-indulge your taste-buds with a healthy regime to keep your body fit.

Your working life

If your creative qualities have been repressed, perhaps because of an early marriage and children, you may feel them coming to the surface once again. You know what you are capable of doing, but feel there has never seemed to be time. This may well be true, but it could also be due to laziness, to becoming too set in a certain routine, or simply to insecurity that has prevented you from getting on with the things you really do want to achieve.

Obviously those with families to bring up cannot suddenly rush off and take up a full time career, forgetting about everything else. But now is a good time to re-examine your original aims and ambitions and to ask yourself if you have attained them. If you have then you are probably satisfied. If you are harbouring a secret ambition then this is the time to be aware of your capabilities, and to search for a way to adjust your life to enable you to use your skills and talents.

If you have been in the same job for years, but have started to feel depressed, dispirited and unfairly passed over when opportunities have arisen, try to analyse the situation. Perhaps it's because you were content to sit back and take second or even third place for so long that now nobody thinks of you as being ambitious. A new environment where you have the chance to start afresh might be just what you have been inwardly hoping for. You've done all your homework, now it's just a question of applying yourself to everything in a much more positive way, which means you shouldn't doubt yourself quite so much. You are more aware of what you expect from life, and even if it is going to take more hard work whoever heard of a Taurean who was afraid of that?

The 25–35 phase

GEMINI

During your early twenties the restless desire to see and do as much as possible may not have completely left you, and perhaps it never will. However, as you approach twenty nine, you may suddenly find yourself stopping dead in your tracks and having to take an objective look at your life so far.

Perhaps you have been so determined to be the social butterfly of the Zodiac that you have spent a great deal of time going from one partner to another, not necessarily getting involved in a deeply emotional way, but somehow searching desperately for mental communication. Don't forget that you may have been expecting too much. Relationships have to be worked at, and perhaps you have always insisted on looking for someone who fitted in with your own aims and aspirations, without bothering to think of changing some of them to blend in with a partner.

Perhaps you got married young, because you had fallen into what you thought was true love, or simply had the urge for something new in your life. Now you are coming up to a time in your life when Saturn returns to the place it occupied at your birth in your horoscope, so you may have to develop a different perspective.

There certainly isn't any need to get in a panic about this, for it's perfectly natural, although it may come as a shock at first suddenly to feel that you don't want to be the same person any more. As a Gemini, you're a past master at change and variety. It may even be that a crisis has appeared in your life at about the same time, or certainly something that could require important decisions being made.

Don't start fretting that everything which has gone before has all been a waste of time. You have been learning necessary lessons all the way. What is happening to you now may seem a little hard to understand, but it will make you aware of the value of life, and with a constructive approach you could become more contented and secure in the future.

Perhaps all that running around for so long has left you realising that what you genuinely want now is to settle down in one place. Your travel can be limited to one or two holidays a year.

A marriage that has suddenly become humdrum and boring can possibly be given a fresh start, if only you are willing to accept that this is a time to streamline your life and to concentrate on improving the things which you have been taking for granted. Perhaps you've been so busy with your own interests over the last few years, you honestly haven't bothered to care if your partner has been happy with you. Don't start thinking about divorce before you have really tried to put some extra effort into making your marriage alive once again.

In many ways this Saturn return can make you feel inwardly free, and therefore far more capable of turning your secret dreams into realities, because at the same time you have also developed the courage to recognize your own limitations.

This new change in your personality, this inward growing up and coming to terms with a great many issues which confused you in the past, is bound to benefit not only you, but those who come into contact with you.

You will probably enjoy a more settled life-style, and may even want to relax with a good book in the evenings, rather than fuss about missing a film which has just opened. An invitation to a cocktail party may go unattended because spending the evening with your family or some close friends will seem more pleasant to you.

Your working life

During this phase of your life, it could be brought home to you strongly that if you have been drifting in your professional life, you want to drift no longer. You may not necessarily want to change the basic direction of your work, but simply to get it onto a more productive level. Whilst writing this I was reminded of an American Gemini friend who was involved in several different aspects of the film business, and travelled all over the world. However, around the time of his Saturn return, when he also had a wife and child to support, he realized that in order to achieve greater success it might be better for him to return to America and take a permanent position with a major company. Saturn's influence paid off well, because he became more creative than before, and wasn't continually running from place to place. He still has a dozen projects in his mind, but has learnt the wisdom of concentrating on just one at a time.

If you're a Gemini housewife who feels bored at home now, and there is someone to look after your children, this could be the time when you decide to take up some part-time work, and give your mind a little extra stimulation. Additional money coming in is always useful. Possessions and creature comforts seem to become more important, and if you haven't been capable of saving in the past, the value of security is bound to be brought home to you now.

The 25–35 phase

CANCER

Have you achieved the goals you were aiming for in both your emotional life and life-style? Or are you becoming restless and taking your bad moods out on the people around you?

It is especially around the period when Saturn returns to the place it occupied in your horoscope when you were born, when you are about twenty-nine and a half, that any little seeds of dissatisfaction seem to grow faster.

However, perhaps some of this is your own fault? Have you been so determined to settle down and create a home that you have shut your eyes and ears to the rest of the world? Is one of your faults to smother loved ones with too much affection?

If you are not yet married, make sure you are not being too pushy with your partner, especially if you are well aware that he or she needs to feel inwardly free. By now you should have learnt how to control your emotions, how to laugh if people make jokes at your expense, and how to stop yourself withdrawing from challenging situations.

Up to now, many thoughts and ideas will have been drawn from experiences close to home. Your childhood will usually have exerted a great influence on you, but now you should start to realize that living your life positively also means standing on your own feet. It's time to make your mark upon the world in the way that you want to do it, and not just because of past conditioning. Don't worry if you start to feel vague insecurities and worries once again. It's natural, especially if you decide that the life-style enjoyed by your parents and grandparents is not necessarily the one that you want for yourself. However, try to realize that accepting certain things just because they were always done that way in the past can be negative. Perhaps because of your exact time of birth you have a Sagittarian ascendant giving you the urge to travel and explore, or a Capricorn Moon inspiring you to soar to the heights of a chosen but as yet unfulfilled career.

This phase in your life is immensely important because it can set the pattern for your future happiness. Don't tie yourself to a daily routine if you feel deep down that it is the wrong one for you, and don't always feel that you have to shoulder everyone else's problems just because you were born with a maternal instinct.

This certainly doesn't mean that if you are blissfully happy in your present existence, you should start to have doubts, for that would be ridiculous. It is simply that around the time of the first Saturn return, you may feel frustrated in some areas of your life, and held back from some of the things you want to do. You will also start to think more constructively about the future, and it is, therefore, a turning point. Perhaps some of your responsibilities will be greater, but inwardly you will be grateful that you have reached adulthood and can no longer be forced into doing things against your will.

If you are happy with everything centred around your home, there is no need to change that simply because you are approaching the age of thirty. One of my clients was once a young and highly successful photographic model, but at thirty she was happier at home looking after her family. Around that time she was offered a new career opportunity as a television actress but decided she was still happier at home.

Once you've made a choice over your future life, don't start having doubts, or regrets, just because a few difficult days happen to come along.

Take the necessary steps to give yourself a healthy body, and don't become someone who moans and groans about the slightest aches or pains or retires to bed at the merest hint of an approaching cold. If you're a typical Cancerian you are house-proud, which means that at least you should get plenty of exercise whilst doing your daily chores. However, laziness can also be one of your tendencies, and you probably find it much more comfortable to sit in front of a huge coal fire reading a favourite magazine than taking the dog for a brisk walk.

Your working life

Dissatisfaction with the way life has treated you work-wise could arise now. If you gave up a promising career because you were in love and wanted to settle down and raise a family, and suddenly you feel envious of friends who do work, you're going to hit out at someone even if it is only yourself.

Besides, if you know that you have the ability to earn your own living at a time when it may be very useful to have some extra money coming in, you may feel even more determined to work, especially if you have some unfulfilled ambitions. Once you have settled down with a family, it is not always easy to combine a full-time career with your domestic life, unless you are able to take on outside help. However, you could find something part-time which fits in with the rest of your day. As you enjoy looking after people, social work or helping out in a hospital could turn out to be perfect. You might even decide to run a little business with a partner who is in a similar domestic situation.

Don't sit back and start moaning to yourself that your working life is over, for it may easily be about to start again in an even more rewarding way.

The 25–35 phase

LEO

Do you still want to rule the world? Are you convinced there is something more to life than you have so far experienced? Has your marriage reached a point where something either has to change radically or you could be heading for the divorce courts? Or have you been leading such a busy social life that the idea of settling down and getting married has not even occurred to you yet?

One of the major effects of the Saturn return which takes place when you are around twenty nine and a half years old, is that you often tend to take a long hard look at yourself, and what you have achieved so far. It may not be an easy time because it will certainly contain its moments of frustration, and perhaps even depression, but it will bring home to you that you have finally reached maturity and that it is time to rid your life of past encumbrances which are holding you back, perhaps through your own fault.

It will also make you realize how important love is to you and that if you want a relationship to work, you will also have to work at it yourself. You can't go through life any more handing out the orders as if you are the only experienced person around. It's fine to want the limelight, but you must also be prepared to share it.

However, if you fell in love when you were very young, and refused to listen to the advice of anyone who tried to tell you that the partner you had chosen was possibly too weak-willed for you, it would be a sad waste of time and energy to keep on moaning about how fed up you are now. For heaven's sake, Leo, don't you realize you have now reached a stage where a realistic and constructive approach to your life is positive and will help you turn past failures into successes, but it is imperative for you to know what you want.

One of your problems is that because of your pride you hate to admit defeat, which can be negative, if it means that having put everything you possibly can into a relationship you shy away from making some firm decisions about ending it. This Saturn return can last up to two and a half years, during which you may go through all sorts of inner conflicts, but you will have valid reasons to feel proud of yourself if you do have the courage to sort out your life and start afresh.

If a relationship which has been giving danger signals for some time does have to end, don't get yourself into a terrible state and behave as if the sunlight has disappeared from your life. It's not usually difficult for you to attract people to your side, just try not to rush headlong into a new involvement only to discover later that you have repeated the same mistake.

Your lifestyle is unlikely to change. You will always want to live as luxuriously as possible, and do a great deal of entertaining. Leos are usually marvellous at presenting smiling faces to the world even on days when they feel down, and they invariably take good care of their health.

Your working life

Hopefully you have now reached a stage in your life where even if you are not the boss, you are respected and carry a great deal of responsibility. If you decided to gravitate to the world of show business, it is unlikely you would be completely unknown.

The Saturn return may have coincided with all sorts of far-reaching decisions in your life, but it is unlikely to have changed your determination to be successful with your work.

However, bossing people about may have seemed like fun when you were younger, but if you become too dictatorial now you will lose a great deal of your popularity. Surely you have realized by now that you are going to get much better responses from your requests by making them in a friendly way and not by roaring at people.

Stop trying to take over the world and changing it to fit in with your own personal aspirations.

You could be such a success if you learnt to apply yourself properly. Until now you may have explored and experimented with avenues in which to express yourself. Maybe you haven't found a suitable niche. Suddenly everything could begin to fall into place with amazing clarity.

You may be happily married with a hard-working husband and a couple of children, and have given up a promising career to look after them, and now the seeds of envy are growing inside you every time you hear anyone talk about their own success.

Come on, stop making excuses for yourself, for if anyone could pick up the threads of a past career, or find something new to do, it's you. You are perfectly able to renew old contacts, to scan the papers for interesting advertisements, or insert one yourself; or you could get together with some like-minded friends and open a small business of your own, just as long as you don't insist on always being the person in charge.

The 25–35 phase

VIRGO

Have you learned to worry less about trivialities? Have you begun to appreciate the so-called good things of life a little more, and stopped expecting everyone else to live up to your ideals? Have you also felt that something is changing almost without your doing anything to effect that change?

By the time you reach your late twenties, you may

have organized your life, although events which take place now may make you realize that even the best laid plans can go awry. You may experience the loss of a relative which has a tremendous effect on you. You may find yourself having matrimonial difficulties, for if you married young, it is often now that the so called "seven year itch" can arise. It is also now that you are experiencing the first Saturn return. Depending on your own personal horoscope this may affect you in various ways, but what it almost certainly will do is to make you bring out your imaginary microscope once again, using it to pinpoint any areas of dissatisfaction in your life.

Up till now your life has in many ways been influenced by your childhood upbringing, but now you are being forced to look upon it in a definitely adult way. You must realize that hanging on to the past can be wasteful and even harmful. It is as if you are being given a choice between a frustrating routine and a more fulfilling destiny.

When Saturn first returns to the place it occupied at your birth, it is sometimes called a time of limitation. It doesn't, however, have to be that. It should also be a time to re-organize your life, and make new plans with greater confidence and optimism.

If you are a typical Virgo, it may still be hard to accept the fact that you are capable of making mistakes. If you have put everything into a relationship and it is not working out, you may have simply cut yourself off inwardly. However, this Saturn return should give you the courage to tackle problems in a positive and productive way by bringing them out into the open and discussing them with your partner.

There is one aspect of your personality which can be both positive and negative, and that is your self-sacrificing quality. It's fine to spend so much time looking after people as long as you are happy doing it, but it is pointless to make a martyr of yourself and be unhappy doing so. I am certainly not suggesting that you should suddenly stop caring for people, or neglect an aging relative, but it is important for you to know why you are doing it, and for it to be fulfilling.

Your responsibilities may sometimes start to seem greater around this time, but learn to give everything the right degree of importance, and don't start worrying unnecessarily.

Think of your life now as if you have come to a crossroads, which provided you make the right choice can lead you towards a more fulfilling future.

If you have not yet settled down, you may now feel that perhaps you have spent too long summing up the various partners in your life, and that what you want more than anything is a settled and hopefully permanent domestic situation. You should certainly be far more aware of your inner needs now, and this could be a perfect time to get married.

You are no longer a child and you simply have to take a more positive approach to life, by making the decisions you feel deep down are important to you, and resolving to eradicate self-doubt and self-criticism from your mind.

If you are happiest being a creature of habit, and your life has so far turned out just the way you hoped it would, then don't feel that I am telling you to turn it upside down just because you have reached a certain age. Without knowing your personal horoscope, it is obviously necessary to generalize, and not every Virgoan is going to reach the age of twenty-nine feeling that change is just around the corner.

It should be good to know, however, that you have reached the stage where you should be perfectly able to take your life in your hands and steer it in the direction you want, without having to ask for someone else's opinion.

Your basic life-style is unlikely to change a great deal. You still need peace and quiet, and companions who don't grate on your nerves. You may never stop worrying completely about minor ailments, but at least you shouldn't be getting in such a flap about them, especially as you now know that moments of relaxation combined with sufficient exercise help to give you a healthy body.

Your working life

Working is unlikely to have presented many problems for you. It's something which many Virgoans almost look upon as a duty, but if you have been putting all your efforts into a career which gives you very little satisfaction, and not even a particularly good salary, it is bound to be around this time that you feel forced to take a closer look at the situation. A creature of habit you may be, but that certainly shouldn't mean pouring all your energy into something which gives you very little in return. Self-sacrifice may be all very well at times, but if you don't want to give yourself ulcers, perhaps you should start to remember your desire to be appreciated and admired. Perhaps you do need to do work which is in some way worthwhile to the rest of the community, but it should be financially worthwhile to you as well.

Change doesn't come easily to Earth signs, but if a full-time job is a necessity, once you reach twenty-nine you must seriously look for the right niche. You are bound to receive good references from your current employment, or even the offer of a promotion once they realize you are planning to leave.

If you gave up work to look after a young family, it won't usually be difficult for you to find something to do, even on a part-time basis. Apart from taking care of people, your secretarial prowess is usually beyond dispute.

The most important thing is for you to be doing something which enables you to start your day optimistically. A Virgoan who sinks into apathy because of a boring job is definitely not being positive, and you may have a lot more work ahead of you in the years to come. You could be marvellous working in almost any field because your ability to spot snags and your logical approach can save a great deal of time-wasting work on impractical schemes.

It is continually being said that Virgo is a born 'server', but at least you should be able to choose who and where you want to serve, especially now.

The 25–35 phase

LIBRA

Many of you will have settled down happily in partnerships by now, but as you approach thirty, you may begin to have doubts and insecurities, and feel that your life is drifting on without a major purpose. This is because once Saturn returns to the place it occupied in your natal horoscope, it often tends to make you feel more aware than ever of what life is all about, and what you want to achieve from now on.

Naturally this doesn't mean that you are going to start screaming "divorce, divorce", walk out of a job, or decide to move to a completely new environment. However, it does mean that you are finally becoming more decisive, and that you are finding it easier to balance your Libran scales which represent the "scales of justice". If you do feel a need for change, at least you would never dream of upsetting the balance in other people's lives unless there was no alternative. If you decide something has to be done about a partnership, you will, therefore, find it much easier to talk things over calmly and tactfully with the person involved before making any final decisions.

However, depending on the actual position of Saturn in your personal horoscope when you were born, this first Saturn return can make you unduly sensitive and even instil in you a lack of confidence. It is therefore vital that you do not let your desire for a peaceful existence allow you to ignore existing problems, hoping they will just disappear.

A marriage or longstanding relationship definitely has to be a joint effort with you. You need a partner who appreciates your endeavours to share his or her life as much as possible. This naturally doesn't mean that you intend to be interfering but you do like to share your partner's problems and to help to find solutions to them. As this characteristic is an integral part of your nature, a partnership which is unequal could become extremely difficult for you to cope with.

Even though you may have been so unsure when making certain decisions for yourself in the past, you sometimes have the unique ability of hitting the nail on the head when it comes to advising someone else on a similar decision. Never lose your ability to see both sides of a situation because when used constructively it is a marvellous gift.

By now you may easily have a young family. Children are often especially important to Librans, who may feel a home is not a complete home without them. Once there are children to look after, it is very unlikely that anyone will be able to accuse you of being lazy, because you often manage to look after everyone and everything at home, and even have a full-time job. So much activity can be fantastic for some of you; and you can usually cope with pressure up to a certain point, but remember that your body needs balance, and never forget to rest when you are tired.

This Saturn return doesn't necessarily mean that you will wake up one morning, deciding it is the right moment to make far-reaching changes. It doesn't happen as quickly as that, and besides that would also be too much of a character switch, unless you have an Ascendant based on your exact time of birth which powerfully affects your Libran Sun.

It would also be generalizing too much to say that all Librans will have settled down in a partnership by the time they reach twenty-five. Some of you may have preferred to follow a different direction in life, especially if you are involved in a career which gives you all the fulfilment you need. However, if you are still living on your own, it could be now that you start to feel the need to share your life with someone on a more permanent basis. Saturn's return can also coincide with the loss of an older relative or friend who was important in your life, which leaves a gap, so that the right partnership is even more vital to you.

It may just be coincidence, but when I think of all my Libran clients and friends, nearly all of them have had either two marriages or two highly important relationships by the time they reached thirty-five. Perhaps this is because you do tend to get seriously involved with someone at a very early age, so that if there are going to be problems, they often come to a head around this Saturn return.

Libra, if you have reached this stage, and decided there are some major steps to be taken, tackle them with confidence. Even though you hate creating upsets, you know you can be tough when necessary. Now, perhaps more than ever, it is necessary to have some direction in your life, and you can't afford to make mistakes.

Your working life

If you are married, because you do like to feel that you are a useful part of your partner's life, you may not necessarily want a full-time career of your own. However, don't forget your tendency to spend excessively, and the chance to have some extra money of your own without having to ask for it could come in very useful.

If you have always enjoyed working, and gave everything up to get married and raise a family, you may start to feel that you have spent a lot of time living in your partner's shadow and that your own talents are being wasted.

Many of you have creative and artistic abilities, and you may even have been developing a flair for interior design by experimenting in your own home, doing some dressmaking, or trying out unusual knitting patterns, so perhaps this could be the moment to see if you can start to do something professionally.

Although Virgo has always been called the "sign of service", you often come a pretty close second, if, by serving, one means helping people. You do want to help, and your basic Libran sense of fair play and harmony at all costs means you want to do something to bring a little more equality to the world.

Some of you may have decided to stay single for this reason, preferring to look after as many people as possible rather than devote all your time and energy to just one or two. Any child with a Libran nanny will certainly be blessed, because she will almost never be ruffled or lose her temper even if her charge is argumentative and obstinate at times.

This Saturn return may coincide with a complete change of career, and often people who didn't necessarily achieve great success before they approached thirty, move on to new heights. If, therefore, you feel it is vital for you to do something more suited to your own particular talents, don't doubt yourself, but begin to be more constructive about finding the right niche.

The 25–35 phase

SCORPIO

If you have reached your mid-twenties and have suddenly begun to realize that although your life may contain its moments of excitement and adventure, in some ways it is beginning to drift on without a great deal of purpose, then if you're a typical Scorpio you won't waste too much time before you do something positive about it.

It's time to make full use of your tremendous insight and powers of analysis and direct them towards yourself.

When you are about twenty-nine and a half years old, and Saturn goes back to the place it occupied in your natal horoscope, it tends to take its toll upon you in one way or another. Saturn may be a hard taskmaster, but an inner need to take a long hard look at yourself and try to sort your life out properly is definitely positive, if done in the right way.

Your co-ruling planet Pluto gives you a great deal of power, and is perhaps one of the major reasons you are considered cold and often ruthless. You certainly don't want to spend the rest of your life with this label so it is time to set the record straight and prove once and for all that you can be as tender and affectionate as any Libran or Pisces.

Around the time of this Saturn return, you may experience an intense feeling of inner loneliness and frustration. This is bound to be especially true if you have concentrated so much on having a good time that suddenly all your old friends have settled down and started to raise families and there you are – intent on playing Casanova to the bitter end.

Those of you who have settled down happily with a loving partner will presumably have learnt to tone down your possessive feelings and to stop being quite so suspicious.

Because of your desire to understand life's mysteries, this Saturn return could make you determined to free yourself of old fears and uncertainties and soar upwards to achieve the destiny you are convinced is your birthright. A true Scorpio almost always has one inherent desire or ambition. It may be to help a partner achieve success, to devote a great deal of time to an important career, to give all the love and support you possess to bringing up your family, or perhaps all three. The main point is that you should realize what you are capable of doing once you know exactly what you are searching for. By the time you are thirty-one, you should have discarded all the negative Scorpio qualities of jealousy, cruelty, ruthlessness and revenge, and realized that it is far better to stick with the positive qualities of the Eagle than those of the insect that stings itself to death.

Always remember that you possess a great deal of courage, and that Pluto's power of regeneration helps you to pick up the pieces and start again even if your life seems to have meandered in the wrong direction. If people you have loved now seem to become old and frail, and even pass away, don't become unnecessarily morbid about death. If a longstanding relationship is faltering and seems to have reached the point of no return, your honesty, self-control and courage will make it imperative to discuss the whole situation with your partner, and to try and resolve problems positively without getting yourself in a terrible state. If you do suddenly find yourself alone at this stage of your life, it is unlikely you will be so for very long. Your magnetic sexual charms can be almost more attractive now. The difficulty won't usually be in finding someone new, but in making sure you have learnt to satisfy your need for a love which is both physical and spiritual, so that you are no longer searching for life's deeper meanings. The natural house of Scorpio in the Zodiac is the Eighth, relating in an almost mystical way to the sexual act and to death, in addition to joint financial and business affairs. However in many ways this "depth" also will imply rebirth, and a "rebirth" is what this Saturn return can bring to you.

Your physical strength is undoubtedly an advantage, and even when you do become ill you tend to have great recuperative powers. However, you should always strive to look after yourself properly and not strain your body with excesses. Remember that life doesn't have to be a continual battle where rest and relaxation are forbidden.

Running a home should present no problems. You enjoy keeping a place neat and tidy and finding the right place for everything, but make sure you don't turn into one of those Scorpios who is continually looking in drawers or pockets when you should be doing the housework.

Your working life

If you chose the wrong job in the past, or are silently brooding because you have been passed over for a promotion you are rightly convinced should have been yours, then for heaven's sake pull yourself together and resolve to do something practical, positive and productive with your working life. Perhaps you never had a specific goal before, but as this Saturn return has made everything clear, you are now determined to make a name for yourself in a chosen field.

If you gave up an interesting job to get married and start a family, it may not be easy for you to do full-time work, but there is bound to be something you could find which will fit in with the rest of your day. Why not apply your enquiring mind to doing some kind of research, or because you enjoy caring for people by helping out in a doctor's surgery. Don't become bored or in any way resentful of your life now so that you start to take your feelings out on other people. It is important that you feel fulfilled, and if a job will resolve your problems, then obviously it is important for you to find one.

The 25–35 phase

SAGITTARIUS

Are you still seeking adventure? Are your mental and physical journeys bringing you the enjoyment and contentment you need, or are you drifting through life rather like a traveller who is unsure of his destination?

You may start to realize that your life has been a great

deal of fun but is plainly leading nowhere. Perhaps you are around twenty-nine years old and have always had a swinging time. You have enjoyed your freedom with no one to answer to and didn't want to settle down. Now you seem to be the odd one out amongst all your married friends. Or perhaps you were a Sagittarian with a Cancer ascendant who decided that marriage and babies were better than freedom any day. Either way, if you *are* feeling dissatisfied with your personal world, once Saturn returns to the place it occupied when you were born it may pinpoint with exactitude the area which could do with some spring cleaning.

This might all come as a bit of a shock to you, but underneath your humorous personality is a serious thinker, and although you sometimes like to trust to luck a little too much, there is surely no way you would take the chance of spoiling your future by not attending to the present? Besides, although Saturn is often associated with limitation, this Saturn return can also bring an inner freedom, a letting go of negative influences and allowing your basically optimistic personality to feel optimistic for the right reasons.

It may not always be obvious that you are as much a Fire sign as Aries and Leo, but you can certainly fall in love just as suddenly as they do. If your romantic life went through some difficult periods in your early twenties, even with perhaps your own subconscious determination to stay uninvolved, don't let past hurts prevent you from being positive about the future. From adolescence into adulthood was one phase, and now you've reached another, because Saturn's return helps to make you wiser and more determined to find the correct niche in the world. By the time you are thirty-one you should know exactly who you really are, where you want to be, and with whom. This is important, because for someone whose interest in religion and philosophy deepens as the years go by, you can be notoriously inept at understanding your own deep needs.

If this learning more about yourself also coincides with the realization that you have grown apart from a partner who was once very dear to you, don't be a coward about discussing the problems, for perhaps he or she is also feeling certain undercurrents in your relationship, and talking things over could bring you closer together again. Naturally the postion Saturn occupied in your own chart is going to affect the way it relates to your particular life, and not everyone is going to go through great emotional changes.

Even if you do decide to settle down and take on a mortgage, your life-style will still be fairly free and easy. You are not noted for your domesticity, but your home is bound to be comfortable and reflect your relaxed personality. A pet certainly wouldn't go amiss if you've lost your wanderlust ways, but don't let this stop you from planning at least one interesting holiday every year.

Your working life

If you started your working life feeling optimistic about your chances of success and have begun to feel you're in a rut, don't think that life is passing you by. Perhaps you have just come to realize that you really need work which will give you more scope to express your creative talents.

Some of you tend to move around regularly, especially if you work in a field which gives you the opportunity to travel. A news reporter or an air hostess might be an ideal occupation for a single Sagittarian who hates to have his or her feet on firm ground for too long at a time.

If you can honestly say to yourself that your present employment does not fulfil you, this Saturn return will probably urge you to be positive about the situation. Don't procrastinate any longer, because with your naturally optimistic personality, and Jupiter's influence, it is unlikely you would be out of work for very long. I remember one client who worked amazingly hard for many years without feeling appreciated. Finally around the time of her Saturn return, which in her personal horoscope had a great bearing on her professional life, she decided to strike out on her own in the same field as her boss and it wasn't long before she was extremely successful.

If you have settled down happily to raise a family, and suddenly miss going out to work, then something part-time or free-lance would be ideal for you. It would give you the freedom to carry on with your other activities, as well as financing some of those trips you may still yearn for.

The 25–35 phase

CAPRICORN

At the beginning of this part of the book, I talked about how Saturn's influence is especially important during this phase of your life.

By now you are aware that Saturn is your own planetary ruler, and perhaps you are secretly fearing that you are going to be singled out for some especially difficult situations now that you are approaching the Saturn return which occurs when you are around twenty-nine and a half years old.

However, you have grown up knowing all about patience, will-power and discipline, and have probably risen above more than a few difficulties in your life.

It has often been said that the first thirty years of your life are the hardest, and that you don't really come into your own until this Saturn return, but now you should begin to feel more optimistic. It is almost as if once you learn to face life more confidently, you suddenly become the child you never were; and if that sounds like double dutch, it is only because you spent so much of your childhood behaving like a little adult that now your fears and inhibitions have subsided, you can laugh at the things which once would have worried you. The picture you have presented to the outside world is one of composure and self-confidence. This Saturn return should help you throw away the last threads of insecurity and become the person people always thought you were, continuing your path up the mountain with a great deal more self-confidence and self-assurance.

For you this Saturn return is almost like the final payment of an old debt, and now your responsibility should be to yourself, and to channeling your life in the direction you are determined it should go. The marvellous part about being a Capricorn is that you don't expect this to happen overnight, because you know full well that what is worth having is worth waiting for.

If you have been so busy working in a chosen career that the idea of committing yourself to a steady relationship or marriage has seemed less important, you may start to realize that what you want more than anything else is a partner with whom to build a future life. You will be more aware of your own deep needs and you will realize that your desire for material security is worthless if you are not sharing your dreams with someone you love, especially if it is someone who will help you to laugh away your blue moods and understand your hidden sensitivity.

You should have more belief in yourself and your abilities by now because you have proved that you can cope. If a marriage or relationship is proving difficult, don't start cutting yourself off from the problems, but get right down to the root of them and don't be afraid to discuss them.

If Saturn is indeed a mythical task master, I have always felt that by using his influence positively we can reap the rewards which life has to offer. Don't be afraid of tackling difficulties, and if you have made mistakes in the past, there is no reason why you should continue to do so.

You will certainly be respected as a parent, but don't be such a stickler for tradition, that in later years you find out that your family were sometimes slightly in awe of you and felt unable to live up to your high ideals.

Your life-style probably won't change now. You're unlikely to develop wanderlust tendencies, unless you have a Sagittarian ascendant! However, if you can afford to pamper yourself with a few more comforts of modern living then do so. If you are busily running a home, being a good wife and mother, and coping with a job as well, don't forget to indulge in some spare-time activities which would also be an aid to relaxation. You should be basically healthy from now on but tension and stress can create problems if they are not checked.

Your working life

If anyone can combine looking after a husband, family and home with a full time career it is you. You seem to do everything so well and positively revel in hard work, looking disdainfully upon those who relax in front of the television after dinner when there are still some chores to be done.

At this stage of your life, if you have continued with a career, it is more than likely you will have become not only successful, but also respected and recognized for what you have done. However, if you are married to a partner who requires your help in some way, even as a behind the scenes figure or a shoulder to lean on, then you will probably be just as happy to play that part, and play it well. The most important factor for you is to provide for a happy and secure old age, since growing older tends to make you feel you could become dependent on others.

If you suddenly have to take a job for financial reasons, remember that your ability to organize people can come in extremely useful.

Whatever you have done so far, this Saturn return will make you feel even more determined to create the right niche for yourself in a working environment. However, if you have built up a successful career or business of your

own, make sure you don't neglect the needs of your close
family in order to follow your chosen path.

The 25–35 phase
AQUARIUS

You should by now have come to terms with your own
personality, and decided whether you want to remain free
in order to follow personal plans and whether friendships
and causes are more important than love and romance.

However, as you approach your late twenties you are
likely to be more at conflict with yourself, because you
are coming up to the Saturn return which takes place when
you are between twenty-nine and thirty years old.

Astrologers tend to consider Saturn, the planet of
discipline, as the co-ruler of your birthsign, together with
the more disruptive Uranus, and this can sometimes be
an especially difficult time for you, with moments when
you feel depressed and full of nervous tension, especially
if you feel hemmed in by your present situation. You must,
however, realize that you are being given an opportunity
to constructively replan your life for a more rewarding
future.

It certainly shouldn't worry you unduly to think that
perhaps changes do have to be made, but you must realize
that Saturn's influence can create limitations and setbacks,
and you have to exercise patience and not expect changes
to occur overnight. It may take up to two and a half
years to find your true path in life, but it can be an exhilarat-
ing time because you should finally realize that you are
no longer bound to the past, and that by resolving to
be more positive there can be a great deal of success ahead
for you.

Your intuition is yet again an added bonus, and you will probably have already sensed that you are coming to a crossroads where it is imperative to take the right direction.

Certain events may affect you now, perhaps the death of a loved one who has influenced you, or an inner loneliness which leads you to search for a closer rapport with one person rather than with a circle of acquaintances.

If you have been happily married for some time and problems suddenly appear, you should have acquired the patience to deal with them calmly. You may also be more aware that your own detachment or erratic ways could have created them in the first place. If you can honestly resolve to be more conscious of the needs of people close to you, you may save yourself many anxious moments in the future. Don't ever allow anyone the opportunity to accuse you of being unfeeling.

Your life-style should never be boring, because it is usually not within your nature to live without sufficient interests to keep you busy. If you are now married with children growing up in your home, there are still bound to be people popping round at odd moments of the day, and you may be involved with local groups or committees.

Remember that you can suffer from nervous tension far too easily if you don't look after yourself properly. Enthusiasm for work is one thing, but sunshine, fresh air and sufficient sleep are usually important for you, whilst Yoga and meditation should certainly help calm your often over-worked mind.

Your working life

Your flair for creative and inventive work should have brought you to a stage where you are happy with the progress you have made so far. However, if things haven't turned out this way and you are going through a period of intense dissatisfaction, try not to become depressed.

Perhaps some of your earlier dreams of success were

too idealistic, and your sometimes unorthodox approach to life meant that a promotion which could have been yours went instead to someone your employer considered to be more reliable simply because he or she was content to take orders without ever questioning them.

Aquarius, you should have learnt by now that non-conformity can be negative, but if you are able to say honestly to yourself that you have done everything possible to prove your worth in your present employment and yet are obviously not appreciated, then you should come to terms with the situation, and look around for something more fitting to your personality.

If you have been busily occupied running a home and looking after a family, and suddenly feel life is passing you by, and you need to work as well, you don't really need advice because you probably know just what you do want to do. Just make sure you don't start neglecting the people closest to you in order to compensate for your own frustrations.

The 25–35 phase

PISCES

Have you been one of those Pisceans drifting with the tide, lacking a true direction. Have you been living in that fantasy world and not affronting those problems which are part of modern life? Have some of your romantic dreams turned into illusion, or are you still convinced there is a great deal to do?

Once you reach twenty-nine and a half, you may start to feel you have not achieved what you expected. This is probably your own fault, for if you are unable to make decisions but prefer to take the easy way out when problems arise, you honestly can't blame anyone else for your dilemmas.

However, you must understand that you have become more realistic and practical about your life by now. The influence of Saturn's return to the place it occupied in your horoscope at birth will reveal to you more than ever any frustrations you may have started to feel. If you married a childhood sweetheart dreaming of a cottage in the country, babies, and happiness for ever, and are now finding that something is sadly missing, you should have the courage to face up to the problem and talk it over with your partner. You must learn that problems don't just disappear, and must be dealt with realistically and decisively. It is not that you suddenly have to change characters and become a hard materialistic person. By all means keep romance in your life, but learn to protect yourself a little more so that other people are not continually taking advantage of you.

You will always be prepared to sacrifice yourself for the people you love, so make sure they are worthy of you. If you are happily married, you are more fortunate than you realize, because your flights of fancy, and sudden changes of mood can make you difficult to live with. Sometimes your children are spoiled simply because you want to do everything possible for them, which often means doing too much, so remember that discipline is necessary for their own good.

You always feel everything deeply, but at this stage in your life, it is vitally important to remember that self pity is negative. Your sense of humour is a great asset, so why not take a more light-hearted look at yourself and realize how much you have to offer to a great many people. The influence of this Saturn return will be constructive, and by the time you have reached thirty-one you should have managed to think of romance with a much more mature approach.

At the risk of offending a few Pisceans, I must point

out that your life-style may be considered inefficient and even lazy by others. However, sweeping dust under the carpet may work for a while, but irritation will set in when your family can't find some of their clothes, or discover those demands for payment of overdue bills. Don't despair though because determined Pisceans can manage to combine successful careers with running well-ordered homes.

Always remember that emotions can play havoc with your health, and that whilst caring for other people is extremely positive, don't ruin your own health in the process.

Your working life

If you have been able to develop your creative talents, perhaps by now you have started to make a name for yourself. But it would be generalizing far too much to imply that every Piscean is going to become an artist, fashion designer or actor. It is important that whichever field you choose to work in you make use of your gifts and also that the surroundings are congenial or you will become discontented and inefficient. The influence of Saturn's return could bring any frustrations to a head, even though it may take two years. If you find dissatisfaction turning into acute boredom and realize that you are achieving absolutely nothing, take a positive approach, and talk to your boss. If this fails, you should admit to yourself that you have chosen the wrong environment, as all the areas of your life must blend together and if your work is a major problem something constructive needs to be done.

However, you must always remember that as financial difficulties seem to beset you throughout your life, it would be ridiculous to take up employment which does not pay enough to give you security. This may be a problem, because you often enjoy helping or looking after the less fortunate.

If you are about to work for the first time, perhaps more to occupy your spare moments than because of the necessity to earn a living, and you don't have any particular qualifications, your unselfish qualities can be put to extremely positive use by doing social or charity work.

WHAT HAVE YOU DONE SO FAR?

... 35–45 and onwards

Are you sure you're mature? Your life should be in order, but is it?

You've been through the first Saturn cycle, and your life in many ways is better organized by now, or at least it should be.

However, some people, once they approach forty, tend to feel "that's it, no more chances". They think they are old, even though they may not look a day over thirty, and once they start to feel that way they are certainly not being positive.

You, on the other hand, should have learnt a great deal about your Sun sign personality, and you ought to be able to cope with most of the problems which arise in your day to day living. You should also have realized that life really can begin at forty. If you have been through lots of different experiences and learnt something from each of them, they should have made you more resilient and even optimistic about what is now in store.

It is, however, a time when you may have to concentrate more on being positive, which can even mean having to tone down some of your basic characteristics. If you are a Leo who is used to being at the centre of everything, and getting lots of praise, it could be your son or daughter who is the star turn now. If you are an Aquarian or Sagittarian who is used to speaking your mind and giving your advice to your children, you may find that they know more than you about certain issues, and that your interference is resented even if they appreciate that it is well meant.

I have heard it said that around the age of thirty-five, discontentment sets in for many people; for a woman it is often when children are growing up and maybe you suddenly feel as if your life is unfulfilled, especially if you gave up a promising career, whilst career women may feel there is something lacking in their domestic lives, and desire more than anything to become a traditional housewife. Men sometimes start to feel the proverbial "seven year itch", or perhaps find certain aspects of their working life are becoming frustrating.

It may be a time when you start to take a second look at your marriage, and wonder if you really can make it work successfully for another twenty years or so. If there has been any kind of infidelity, a situation could come to a point of no return, and not withstanding any pangs of remorse, it may be decision time again. However, if you understand the characteristics of your Sun sign you should be in a strong position and well able to weather any storms. The rest of your life can be immensely rewarding if you are now able to have more faith in your ability to take decisions which are important to you and to the people who are closest to you.

Perhaps finally you have learned to be the person you always wanted to be.

35–45 and onwards

ARIES

If you have learnt all your lessons properly, you will not have lost your zest for life. You will hopefully have been taking it at a steadier pace though, and not be quite so determined to take over the world and run it your way.

Your qualities of leadership remain, but they should not exasperate other people quite so much. Could it really be true, have you finally started to understand the meaning of that one little world "patience"? Unfortunately, this may not always be so, for "I want it now" is a phrase I even heard recently from an eighty-one year old Arien.

However, you shouldn't be falling headlong into unrealistic love affairs quite so often. It's more likely to be lasting friendships and relationships which mean the most to you now.

You seem to be becoming more like your opposite sign of Libra, with the need for balance and harmony in your life. Don't worry, the Aries ram isn't turning into a sheep, you will never lose your enterprising and adventurous spirit even if it is a little tamer now.

You should also be learning at last that there really should be a time and place for everything, and that losing your temper in a room full of people simply because they don't agree with you is certainly not going to gain you the respect you desire.

However, what *have* you done so far? You certainly shouldn't be feeling in a rut, as a typical Arien couldn't exist for long in the wrong situation, and you would have extricated yourself from it in one way or another. You shouldn't be afraid of "middle age", for who ever heard of an Arien who didn't rise to a challenge, and isn't that what middle age can be? Look at yourself in the mirror, don't you look younger than your years? You can still get up at the crack of dawn, run a household with demanding offspring and a husband insisting on gourmet meals, whilst continuing with a full or part-time job, and have half a dozen other interests too. Mars, that God of War, helped to give you your inner strength, and now that you use it in a positive way by toning down your "me first" attitude, your days should be much easier to cope with.

If there are problems in your marriage or a longstanding relationship during this period, don't be afraid to discuss them with your partner, but do so calmly and rationally, rather than blurting everything out in an inopportune moment.

Longfellow's words "Something attempted, something done, has earned a night's repose" often apply to you. You probably don't sleep well if your life isn't in order, but don't forget that you may not always be able to sort things out overnight, and patience may once again be necessary.

The right domestic environment is often more important to you now, together with a more tranquil life. Blazing the trail for others to follow is all very well, but now you may need to feel the security and contentment you subconsciously yearned for when you were a child.

Your working life should also be more settled, although if you are convinced you have never made full use of some specific talents, explore all the avenues, and don't deny yourself the chance to fulfil yourself in your chosen field. Stimulation in your work will always be of great importance to you.

You will probably never lose your streak of extravagance when you have money in your hands, and hopefully an accountant or bank manager has guided you from an early age so you have no unnecessary problems now.

You should have accepted finally that thinking before taking action is usually the right course for a fiery Arien; Your health should certainly be the better for it. Of course you are still likely to have those visits to the dentist, and you're bound to get the occasional headache if you overwork your Aries head too much. However, if you remember to allow yourself some relaxing moments and put aside the worries of the world, letting a little peace and harmony pass over you with your favourite piece of music, or simply take a snooze in a comfortable chair, your health and fitness should make you proud of your birthsign.

You shouldn't have been defeated by anything yet, Aries, so remember that the rest of your life can be something to look forward to optimistically, especially if you have finally learnt to tone down some of the characteristics which used to annoy the people closest to you.

Hopefully you will also have accepted that "patience" isn't just a boring word invented to spoil your fun, but that it can be a positive influence too.

35–45 *and onwards*

TAURUS

Are you suddenly feeling in a rut and don't like it? Could it possibly be your own fault? Didn't you heed any warning signals which flashed into your mind when you were around twenty-eight or twenty-nine? Did you just go along doing everything the way you had always done before, woke up one morning, found it was almost your fortieth birthday, and suddenly felt neglected as if life has been passing you by?

On the other hand you might equally be blooming into, what everyone tends to call "middle age", in a happy and contented way. You may not have any great desire to create changes in your life. Perhaps you've seen enough of your friends going through crisis after crisis, and you are well aware that life does not necessarily turn out the way that people hoped it would. If you are feeling older, you are probably feeling wiser too. Your patience and determination have invariably helped you to overcome any difficulties, and you don't want to create any unnecessary dramas in your life now.

If you are feeling any unrest, or uncertainty, because events outside your control are changing your life, then don't start to become too worried. Your placid personality has helped you until now, so there is no reason for you to begin doubting your strength of mind to rise above problems.

I have said before that Taureans hate to be pushed into

doing anything, you like to make up your own minds, and you certainly don't like having to do that in a rush, but life doesn't always give you this luxury. You should have realized by now how lucky you are. You don't usually make mistakes by taking impulsive decisions like many Ariens, you're not usually a great worrier like lots of Virgoans, you're just a persistent, resolute Taurus! It's probably true that you still won't let anyone force you into anything you are totally against, but at least you are more prepared to see the other person's point of view, and slowly, very slowly you even come round to the realization that they could even be right.

You should have a whole new world to look on since you learned to have more faith and inner security. If you have children, you should be gaining a great deal of pleasure seeing them grow up; and your life-style will probably include a house or flat with access to a garden, where your green fingers can be kept busy.

When Saturn returned to its original place in your birth-chart, it should have given you the courage to take some long hard looks at yourself and to do something constructive with your life. You should feel much happier now. You will probably have taken the opportunities you wanted and channelled your mental and physical energies into the direction you always wanted to go.

Now you've reached this stage in your life, you've learnt that over-eating can play havoc with your figure, that getting caught out in the rain without an umbrella can give you a cold which goes straight to your throat, that refusing to meet some friends because you're more comfortable lazing around at home can make you unpopular. You should have learnt to unbend a little when necessary, but to continue to stand firm by your principles if you are convinced about them.

You are not usually anxious to alter the pattern of your working life unless a situation is thrust upon you. You were almost certainly settled in your chosen career by the time you were thirty, but if you do have to make a move, then for heaven's sake don't panic. You are never going to lose those capable qualities which make you so important to have around. You will also never lose your capacity for hard work, and even if for a while you have to do something which isn't especially enjoyable, you will rise above it.

Taurus is known as "the builder" of the Zodiac, and even if the foundations of your life at times do seem a little shaky, you're bound to have been building up your security over the years with your clever handling of financial affairs, and you are unlikely to suddenly start to develop an extravagant streak now.

Taurus − you have nearly always known where you were going in life, so make sure that your patience and practicality continue to be used in positive ways, and enjoy the sights, sounds and feelings so necessary to your senses, but never ever give anyone the opportunity to say "Taurus is a boring sign" again.

35−45 and onwards   

GEMINI

It may not seem so long ago that you came to a crossroads in your life, and having reached the early thirties, finally realized that life could be very satisfying without running around in circles.

You should certainly be more aware of the relationships you want in your life now. If an earlier marriage failed, perhaps you even decided that you would prefer to keep your involvements on a less emotional level. Certainly as a Gemini, it's unlikely you would ever be short of company.

Or perhaps you have finally come to terms with all

the things you hoped your marriage would be, and decided that the company of the one person who has at least made an effort to understand your personality, and live with your constant changes of moods and ideas, was worth more than anything in the world to you.

It's not that you're willing to settle for less, but deep down you now know that a continual agitated search for something elusive can be unrewarding. Besides you are usually an expert at adjusting yourself to environments, and you should be wise enough to know that being mature doesn't mean taking a rest in the afternoons or confining yourself to a wheel-chair.

You must never forget that your ruler, Mercury, was the winged messenger of the Gods. Your own Gemini wings still need to fly and there are bound to be new horizons to discover. Hopefully you are now much better at scheduling your days, and managing to give yourself the right amount of relaxation, and certainly, with your quicksilver mind your interest in life isn't going to waver. A friend of mine's Gemini mother is in her late seventies now, but it's not so long ago that she set off by train across France to see some pre-historic cave drawings.

Your working life should now be more settled, with perhaps it's greatest successes yet to come. I can't believe that it is simply coincidence, that whilst planning this book I heard about two friends, one working on a newspaper, the other on a magazine, each of whom was offered an editorship. Needless to say, they were both over thirty-five, both Geminians, and both married with children.

If you're at home, and your children are growing up, you may need something to stimulate your Gemini imagination, so why not turn all your positive attributes, those of being a wonderful sales person, a good talker, a clever decorator, an originator of ideas, into something really constructive? Make your life continue to work around you. Do something you enjoy which can fit into your domestic schedule, and you will feel even more alive.

You may not have accumulated a great deal of money over the years. Geminians usually like to spend, but at least you have probably made sure you have sufficient to cater for all your varied interests. If you haven't, then don't worry too much about it, for you certainly won't have lost either your adaptability or your versatility. Put these to good use now, find the right niche, and earn a little pocket money.

Be on your guard for touches of rheumatism which might creep into your joints with the years, and always remember that sufficient relaxation is important for your nervous system. This doesn't mean reading into the early hours of the morning if you can't bear to put down a fascinating book. Never forget that it's sometimes far too easy for you to be an insomniac, and a busy person needs to have enough sleep.

What *have* you been doing up to now Gemini? You're bound to have crammed a great deal into your life since you first aimed inquisitive questions at your parents and teachers, but if you are still not satisfied with everything you have achieved, perhaps this is the moment to arm yourself once again with one of these blank sheets of paper, and list your objectives as of today. There are bound to be almost as many as when you did it the first time.

Gemini, you should have learnt by now that being positive doesn't simply mean having an ability to talk your way in and out of situations at your will, for that can turn into a negative characteristic and mean that you have developed a selfish streak. On the other hand it doesn't have to mean giving up interests which have always been important to you. It means learning to slot them into the right place, and to always make sure you are aware of your priorities.

35–45 and onwards

CANCER

You may be in your element with the perfect domestic set-up around you, and it is now that you should be able to relax and enjoy some of the comforts you deserve, because you usually put a great deal of effort into everything you do.

However, it is also now that the moods of depression which Astrologers tend to associate with your sign could affect you more. Perhaps you are far too aware of the years creeping up, and perhaps you didn't heed the warning notes when Saturn's influence urged you to sort the dead wood out of your life.

As a Cancerian, it is unlikely that you will be completely happy if your emotional life is not giving you enough satisfaction. If therefore some of your "down" moods have begun to reach an all time low, you obviously know something must be wrong.

This is an important phase in your life, the one thing you mustn't do is start to bury your feelings without talking about them. If you have been encountering any matrimonial problems, summon up the courage to discuss the situation with your partner, or first talk things over with a trusted friend if it seems easier that way. Hiding your emotions once again under your shell may seem to be an easy way out, but is only likely to make the matter worse.

Perhaps you have been so pre-occupied with being "a perfect home maker" that you have spent almost too much time in your own surroundings, and have in some ways lost touch with the rest of the world. It may therefore be necessary for you to broaden your horizons and become more involved with outside interests, especially if you feel that you have begun to grow apart from your partner and not kept up with his or her interests.

Once you are over thirty-five, it would be wonderful to think that you could live happily ever after in a kind of Utopia, but life isn't Utopia, and unfortunately this is a time in your life when past mistakes can catch up with you, and regrets for things gone by can take up far too much of your time and energy. It is, therefore, even more important to try and look at the positive side of life, and even if you do feel hurt inside, to give other people the impression that you are self-assured and determined enough to rise above any problems.

If you have children, you should certainly enjoy watching them grow up, and being around to take care of their needs. However, once your son is old enough to think of taking a partner, you don't want him to feel that no one else could possibly live up to his expectations of what a woman should be, simply because you were always so perfect, do you? Or for your daughter to be subconsciously looking for a father figure with her very first boyfriend? Learn to let your children grow up and fend for themselves, perhaps remembering the words of a certain Comtesse Diane de Poitiers, who wrote "to spoil children is to deceive them concerning life; life itself does not spoil us".

Your home and family will invariably be the focal point of your life, even if you are involved in a career. However, learning to let go of the past should perhaps be a continuing lesson for you. Don't stick so closely to your symbol of the crab that you cling tenaciously onto people and possessions long after you should.

If you have no children, or if they have grown up and left home, and if for one reason or another you are living alone, you don't need to feel lonely, because it shouldn't be difficult for you to lead an active social life, and you could also bestow some of your inherent warmth and tenderness on a pet.

Your health will often depend a great deal upon the way you feel emotionally, but once you are over thirty, it is also important to watch your weight and make sure you are not eating too much stodgy food. Remember that the breast and stomach areas are particularly related to your sign, and that some of you may also be ulcer prone.

You are unlikely to have changed jobs very often. Your desire for security means you are prepared to work hard in return for a fair salary. If you run a business, because of your efficient methods of organization, your profits should be giving you satisfaction now. Financially, you are unlikely to over-extend yourself, although you should make sure that your sometimes childish trust in the people you care for doesn't lead you into situations where your generous nature is taken advantage of.

Never let yourself slide back into the past, Cancer. Don't just say, "Well, I've achieved lots of good things in my life so far, let's just wait and see what happens next". It is all very well to have a treasure chest of memories, but you have a life ahead of you too. Besides it's your responsibility to make everyone forget once and for all that Cancerians are often moody and detached, for you should have learnt by now to smile more and show them the new, optimistic and positive you.

35–45 and onwards

LEO

One marvellous factor about being a Leo is that no matter how old you are, you hardly ever lose your enthusiasm and self-assurance.

Having experienced the first Saturn return, you should have come to terms with many aspects of your personality, and realized that it is often necessary to take second place in order to live happily in the world. If you have been fighting against this, and if you have children growing up in your home, it will probably be made clear that, although your importance is certainly not to be under-estimated, you may not always get the attention you think you deserve. You may not appreciate hearing this, but to take second place is actually good for you, and you should have learnt to accept it long before now.

However, one strange Leo characteristic is that you tend to worry unnecessarily about your appearance and about what other people really think of you, which certainly doesn't tie in with your image. Once you reach thirty-five, you do sometimes become more unsure of yourself, usually at the end of an unsatisfactory marriage or relationship, when you feel your life is going downhill.

There is absolutely no reason why your emotional life should collapse once you pass thirty-five, far from it, for emotional ties can be even more rewarding if you will allow yourself to be taken in hand once in a while. You will start to blossom more if you allow your positive qualities of sincerity and generosity to take precedence over any bossy, intolerant or patronizing mannerisms which may still be with you.

I remember a Leo client who married someone with a rather weak personality when she was very young. She had a fairly difficult marriage which produced a son, and after an inevitable break-up, went through all kinds of depressions, saying her life was finished and that she would never marry again. Once she realized her life wasn't over just because of one mistake, and once she listened to some advice, she relaxed and began to regain her original sunny personality. Soon enough she met someone new, but because he was younger, an overdose of Leo pride prevented her from revealing her age. They fell in love and eventually married and when she did finally disclose her age, it didn't change a thing. Don't have too much pride, Leo, learn to be more honest with yourself and accept that you have your vulnerable spots just as people born under other signs have theirs.

Perhaps this is the moment to tell you that even when you come up against seemingly impossible odds, you tend to have a saving grace. Your courage is enormous, and you will usually do anything possible to protect yourself and the people you love. Your children will soon realize that although at times your discipline may be strict, you love them deeply, and will do all you can for them.

This courage will help if you have suddenly reached a point when you feel something has to change and that you are the only one who can create the change. However, with all your self-assurance and pride, it can also sometimes take you too long to do something constructive about a negative situation, which means that you end up wasting time and energy.

Your pride in your home will not diminish as the years go on. If anything you may enjoy entertaining even more. You will also tend to appreciate an active life, for although you may have occasional bouts of laziness, keeping fit and healthy are often second nature to you.

As you get older, you could have occasional aches and pains, especially in your back. It would also be wise to remember that because Leo also rules the heart, you shouldn't start racing around like a twenty-year-old once the years creep up. However, that, of course, is something your own doctor will be able to advise you on by knowing your personal case history.

If the Saturn return coincided with a change in your working life, the chances are that you may have not only started something new, but managed to achieve a great deal of success in the intervening years. You are especially good at building up a company, and may have employees of your own by now.

If you have been content to let your life revolve around your home and family, you may need something new to fulfil your spare hours now, especially if your children have begun to lead their own lives in homes of their own. What better opportunity than to put your capable and enterprising Leo mind to work, and to find something worthwhile and interesting to do. It is unlikely that you will have lost your extravagant tastes, and think how useful it will be to have some extra money coming in. Don't worry if you can't work full-time, find yourself something part-time, where your ability to organize and be creative can be put to good use.

Never moan that life has passed you by without giving you a chance to be in the limelight. It simply isn't in your nature to give up, besides don't forget you are a Lion. You often have more courage than the rest of us. Even if your own little world tumbles down around you, no one is more adept at picking up the pieces and starting again than you.

You have a great deal to contribute to life, and if you have managed to tone down the sometimes over-powering side of your nature, other people should be encouraged to realize what happiness they can have by being as warm-hearted and enthusiastic as you; and then, Leo, you certainly will have something to be proud of, and in your own special way you will be a star.

35–45 and onwards

VIRGO

Once you have reached this stage of your life you should have finally learnt that needless worrying is not only an incredible waste of time and energy, but can also play havoc with your nerves.

When Saturn returned to the place it occupied in your horoscope at birth, it gave you an opportunity to take a long and discriminating look at your life, and to do something constructive about anything you were dissatisfied with. Life should be smoother sailing now, especially if you have come to terms with the descriptions astrologers tend to give of you – fussy, critical, analytical, a server – and resolved that if these characteristics are really yours, at least you will never use them in a negative way.

However, if you are one of those Virgoans who has always been afraid to show strong feelings, and bottled your emotions up for years and years, once the forties approach you could go through a crisis of a different kind. The frustration and desire for something different which affects many people in their late twenties may only now be affecting you.

You may have been content to remain in the same situation or you may have been so busy taking care of everyone else's problems for all these years that you have almost forgotten about your own needs.

If there is something bothering you, it is essential that you do something positive about it. It really isn't good for you to suppress your feelings. Emotionally you tend to be a conventional person, and there are certain things you hold sacrosanct, such as marriage and the family, but if you do come to a crossroads in your life around this time, then do approach it with a positive attitude. Don't shut away those feelings into a corner of your mind hoping you will be able to ignore them and get on with the rest of your life. Perhaps every Virgo needs someone to confide in without the fear of being laughed at, because the doubts and insecurities which worry this sign often appear trivial to a more extrovert sign.

However, you can give everyone else a few shocks when it comes to finally discovering yourself. I remember a Virgo client who on the surface was a cool and reticent lady married for years to the same man, and all their friends thought they were blissfully happy. Suddenly she left him, seemingly out of the blue, although in fact problems had actually been brewing for years, and she had simply tried to ignore them and patch things up. Many people blamed her, and she did nothing to cover up the rumours which flew around the neighbourhood. As a Virgo, you are probably just as long suffering, but a point may come when you feel you must make changes and find the courage to re-plan your life. If this happens, never blame yourself unnecessarily. Stop being the critic for once in a while and learn to consider yourself a little more.

If you don't make sure your life is running smoothly now you run the risk of being more disgruntled later on. Nothing is worse than a person who constantly harps on previous mistakes and criticizes past and present friends, yet does nothing constructive to improve things. If you want to make a martyr of yourself and continually take on extra responsibilities, then keep quiet about it, and remember you more than likely had a choice.

As a parent, it is not always easy for you to be highly demonstrative with your love, but if you craved for affection as a child, never let your own children feel you don't care enough about them. You sometimes carry your critical assessments a little too far and upset people unnecessarily.

Try not to be one of those overly fussy parents who can make a child rebel in later years. It may not be easy to go to sleep whilst your teenage daughter is at the local disco with some friends, but you have to realize that your parents probably went through the same experiences when you were young, and trying to confine someone else's life to fit in with your own ideals can be selfish.

A spick and span home will always be your desire, but do try to relax your strict rules of tidiness if you have children growing up around you. It won't hurt if things are not put back exactly in their places every single day. Besides you owe it to yourself to relax more now. You've usually worked hard for most of your life in one way or another, and it's about time you let other people help you, even if you do feel as fit as a twenty-year-old.

However, being idle doesn't come especially easy to a Virgo, and if you are a housewife with time on your hands you might easily decide to take up some work which can fit in with your domestic life. If you were a teacher or nurse when you were younger, there could easily be an opening for you again.

With your marvellous powers of concentration and your efficient manner, you are bound to be successful in your working life now. It is however important to make sure you are not taken for granted in any way, or overlooked when promotions are in the air. You are unlikely to suddenly become a spendthrift, but you know that you always do feel safer if there is some spare cash to put away for the future.

It is time to broaden your outlook, especially if you have spent too many hours worrying about trivialities in the past. Life still has a great deal to offer you, and you should now be shrewd enough to realize it.

Don't give anyone the chance to detect you fussing unnecessarily about your health or making mountains out of molehills ever again. You should have given yourself a new image by now, and learnt that being positive should also mean that when you look at yourself in a mirror you appreciate what you see, and I don't mean just physically.

35–45 and onwards

LIBRA

Have you managed to achieve the perfect balance which Librans usually strive for? Do you have a partner who understands you, and people you enjoy looking after? Are you taking good care of your health?

You have passed the Saturn return and hopefully organized your life constructively. If changes were necessary you should have had the courage and will-power to make them, and be feeling far more settled and secure by now.

However, life doesn't always work out as you would have planned it and this could be the time when people close to you may be re-organizing their own lives in some way and you feel left out.

Suddenly you may discover that your previous ability to see both sides of every situation is not so easily exercised when applied to your children who have problems of their own to resolve. Perhaps your partner is going through some kind of crisis and you feel you just don't have the energy to cope with everything. If this does happen it may simply mean that you have not followed the advice which is so necessary to your sign, that of never giving way to excesses. It doesn't matter whether it is food, drink, too much exercise, even too much rest, if you don't learn to take them all in the right amounts, you are going to make life more difficult for yourself.

By now you should certainly realize that you have an unfair advantage on the rest of us. You often manage to look more youthful than people of other signs who could even be many years younger than you. If you have started to feel sorry for yourself, then a perfect pick-up for you could be a quick look in the mirror.

As a parent you sometimes devote so much time to your partner that the needs of your children may be overlooked, although this is certainly not to say that you ever mean to be intentionally neglectful.

Libra, if problems did arise in the past and you hesitated to bring them into the open, deciding to drift on because the idea of change worried you too much, try not to continue in the same vein now. You must realize that your ability to charm people and make friends easily will not be lost, and will almost always ensure that you will never lead a solitary existence unless you choose to. You should therefore never be afraid of taking steps that may seem drastic because they involve cutting off a longstanding relationship. You don't do things lightly, but never forget that because you are an idealist and perfectionist, your Libran scales will swing from side to side far too often if they are not balanced properly.

This is also a time when a partnership can bring you greater contentment and happiness than ever before, especially if you have worked hard at it over the past years. It is unlikely you have suddenly turned into a difficult and demanding person, and therefore there could be a great deal of emotional security to enjoy.

You have always delighted in making your home surroundings as bright and comfortable as possible; your enjoyment in doing so will not diminish as the years go on. If anything, you will find it even more important to live in harmonious surroundings, and although you may have been developing an untidy streak over the years, you certainly want as much comfort as possible now.

Your health will always depend on how you have been looking after yourself. Don't forget that kidney complaints can flair up very easily in people born under your sign. If you did not study yoga when you were younger, you may decide to do so now, and it will certainly help to calm you and give you the inner harmony which is so important to your sign. Walks in the country, enjoying the fields, trees, flowers and birds will be invaluable for calming your nerves.

In your working life you could be making quite a name for yourself now. You may not have aspired to be a leader, but you have probably always enjoyed praise and admiration. You make a perfect boss because of your ability to be fair and understanding, and when you are involved with the public in any way at all your tact and diplomacy should certainly never be underrated.

If you gave up work a long time ago because of your family, and are now beginning to feel restless, try to think of something you can do even on a part-time basis. Remember your ability to help people. I know one Libran who, when her children started to grow up, decided to offer a service to people who had to leave their homes empty, and needed someone to feed the cat, deal with the post, and generally see that things were kept running smoothly. It started off in a small way, but it wasn't long before it became immensely successful. Soon she had to take on a partner, which made her even happier, since not too many Librans like working completely alone. It made her feel more fulfilled, and her marriage and home life became even better as a result.

Libra, you should no longer have to worry about what might happen in the future. You should have learnt to overcome your hesitancy each time anyone required a decision from you. Don't lose your sense of fair play, but make sure you never let those scales slip too far one way or the other. Forget about procrastination, and let "being positive" be your aim from now on.

35–45 and onwards

SCORPIO

Have the mysteries of life been made clearer to you now? Have you learned to blend your desires for physical satisfaction with the mental and spiritual communion which is also necessary? Or have you constantly made sacrifices to such an extent that you suddenly see the years slipping away and are becoming frightened that life is unfairly passing you by?

To a Scorpio, approaching forty can be a somewhat sobering thought, especially if you have relied too much on your sex appeal and magnetic personality in the past. A positive attitude is now very necessary, and that is surely something you should have been learning all along. Growing older may worry you only in terms of your appearance, because you don't usually fear death – if anything some of you seem to have an almost morbid interest in the subject, or develop a strong interest in reincarnation and spiritualism. Now, as never before, you really should endeavour to balance your life so that it will be satisfying on every level.

If you are happily settled in a marriage which has mellowed through the years and your children are growing up around you, make sure you are not turning into an overly possessive mother and preventing your children from trying to lead their own lives. Just think back – remember how you hated anyone behaving the same way with you? However, don't go to extremes and be like a Scorpio I once knew who was far more concerned with fulfilling her own personal life than bothering about the needs of her offspring, to the extent that they had no one around when they needed to talk about some of the normal childhood problems associated with growing up. You may have needed some guidance and direction in your own childhood, so make sure you are prepared to hand out some to others now.

Scorpio, you definitely need a reason for living, and whether it is your family, a job, or something else, it has to make you glad to be alive when you open your eyes each morning. You have tremendous staying power, and by now your natural instinct will probably have developed to such an extent that you do not often need to be told what you should be doing with your life? Having to learn the hard way through past mistakes should not have taken away your determination to rise above any negative qualities which could still exist.

You should have learned to calm down, and not to transmit such powerful undertones of energy. Try to be more like a tranquil Libran. Even if you desperately believe in something and want to convince everybody else about its values, don't be quite so intense. You must have understood by now how exhausting it can be for your listeners.

You will always be proud of your home. Even without a great deal of money, you will be determined to see that not only is it as comfortable as possible, but that you still have your own private little domain.

If you haven't worked for years, and it suddenly becomes obvious that the housekeeping budget is becoming impossible to cope with, no sacrifice will be too great for you to make where your family is concerned. Not only will you cut out as many non essential items as possible from your shopping list, but you will probably resolve to get yourself a job of some kind. It is far better for you to behave this way, because a Scorpio who is unhappy with his or her surroundings can start to become extremely discontented and resentful even if it doesn't show on the surface.

If you have a career, by now you have probably shown more than a few people that when a Scorpio aims for a certain goal, others had better watch out. However, perhaps you have had to make a great many sacrifices along the way, long hours, having to cope with difficult people, even cutting short your holiday when it was necessary. Remember you cannot continually overwork your body without allowing it some time off. Hopefully now you are able to relax a little more, and not drive yourself at too hectic a pace.

Scorpio, you who are so concerned with delving deeply into the secrets of life, probably remain a mystery to a great many people who think they know you. You still hide some of your deepest emotions beneath the surface of your personality, and even if that personality has softened over the years, there could still be an underlying ruthlessness to be brought out at will.

Hopefully, you are not still searching earnestly for a person or ideal to give you the proof that life is worthwhile, because if you are really prepared to continue developing the positive characteristics of your sun sign, life should continue to bring you the necessary excitement, happiness and fulfilment in the years to come. Always remember to show how loyal you can be, and help to make people forget all about the "sting in the tail" of a Scorpion.

35–45 and onwards

SAGITTARIUS

There is a touch of Peter Pan about your sign. The years may affect many people, but not you. I can think of one seventy-six-year-old lady who has more vitality and energy than a few thirty-year-olds born under different signs! Of course this is generalizing, but it should certainly help to reassure you that life is not over at forty, but indeed could be starting afresh.

If the Saturn return coincided with a desire to clip your Sagittarian wings and stay on terra firma, you could now be enjoying a contentment and security you never experienced when you were more interested in coping with your life as if it was the Grand Prix. Even if your desire for excitement and adventure has diminished, you will be just as interested in discovering more about the world as you ever were. You will also become even more philosophical when you reach your late thirties.

However, you must watch your tendency to moralize, or to become too narrow-minded and bigoted. Remember that nobody likes to be criticized and disapproved of, and if it is a habit which you have formed over the years, try to come to terms with it now.

If you have children growing up in your family, be extra specially understanding. And if you have a sensitive Cancer or Pisces child, it really is important not to upset them with your outspokenness. You may not be as authoritative as Leo but you can sometimes come a close second, with your determination to force your will and opinions on everyone.

Sagittarius, surely at this stage of your life you haven't forgotten your own deep need for freedom, so don't try to keep your family on an invisible chain even if at times you feel lonely and would like to be surrounded by company.

If you are encountering problems or unhappiness, don't feel that you should cling on to your marriage or relationship because of a fear of being lonely, but bring these difficulties out into the open. Your judgement is usually good enough to enable you to find the right moment, and provided you manage to choose your words carefully, you should be able to clear the air.

Mental communication becomes even more important to you as you grow older. This doesn't mean that someone who has always enjoyed the lighter side of life is suddenly going to turn into an intellectual overnight. If you were able to travel in your youth, you may find yourself reading more and more about the places you would still like to visit even if for financial reasons you are unable to do so.

Perhaps you are a Sagittarian who has been through a broken marriage and you don't want to risk another. Have you forgotten your asset of being able to look upon life as an adventure in spite of setbacks? This should have made you more perceptive and less rash, so don't lose that positive attitude.

Your life-style isn't necessarily going to change now. You may still dislike having to cope with domestic chores, this is considered a Sagittarian characteristic, but if you are like two Sagittarian friends of mine you may have developed an interest and skill in carrying out every conceivable do-it-yourself job around the home.

Fresh air is always important to you, so sport or taking the family pet for a brisk walk will invariably make you feel good. As you get older you could be prone to a touch of rheumatism or sciatica, begin to suffer from pulmonary complaints, and if you have suddenly started to eat and drink excessively, discover a liver problem.

If your career has been steady, you have probably made quite a name for yourself by now, but never forget that a free-lance activity will always prove to be especially congenial to your sign. If you find you have more time on your hands now that your family is growing up, then don't be afraid to take a chance and perhaps turn one of your hobbies into something even more productive. You may find your skills make you perfect as a translator, or part-time teacher, whilst if you have neighbours who have to leave their pets alone all day you might even start up a dog walking service. You invariably love animals and being out in the open, so it could be a perfect job for you!

If you are financially sound, do be careful that at this stage in your life you don't start to gamble. I'm not suggesting that you are going to rush off to the nearest Casino and start playing black-jack whenever you are free. However, with too much time on your hands you might just be tempted to recklessness.

Sagittarius – we would be lost without your bright and cheerful remarks when the rain is pouring down outside and everything looks grey and miserable.

If you really have learnt to make the most of your sun sign, you should have also realized by now that being positive also means that you cannot simply organize the rest of the world to fit in with your own ideas, and that to be completely happy and fulfilled, it is necessary to let other people have their say.

As the years go by and you find yourself becoming more philosophical, you will realize the occasions when you tend to want to dominate others. This new awareness combined with your sense of humour should enable you to suppress these feelings and instead resolve to keep up the cheerful, adventurous image expected of you.

35–45 and onwards

CAPRICORN

Does that mountain peak seem any nearer? Do you feel fulfilled? Perhaps you are wondering if you gave yourself a harder task than necessary in planning your life, and now discover that you feel slightly envious of your more light-hearted and less materialistic friends?

One marvellous aspect about being a Capricorn is that you may now start to develop more of a sense of humour, and if you will also allow yourself to relax and be more positive, your life will become even more enjoyable. You are not quite so concerned with the outward trappings of material success, and know yourself that much better.

However, there is no doubt that you are one of the true workers of the Zodiac in every sense of the word, and at this stage of your life, it would be pleasant to think you can afford to be less concerned about the future.

Your self-confidence should certainly have increased, because it should be obvious to you that whereas some people sadly go downhill in looks and appearance as they approach middle age, you, on the contrary, seem to positively bloom. Capricorn women develop a new elegance, whilst men born under this sign seem to become even more debonair once they approach the forties.

You have probably spent a great many years doing certain things because you felt they were your duty, and perhaps some of them were genuinely necessary. You will be well aware now of the fact that emotional fulfilment is as much your right as anyone else's.

If you have drifted away from a partner because you were involved in a career or caring for your family, it can sometimes be hard for you to admit that something has gone wrong and needs facing up to. Saturn's influence often does seem to make you far tougher on yourself than you would be on someone else in the same situation, and finding it sometimes difficult to express your emotional feelings in the right way can make it even harder. However, you are still a stickler for a solid conventional life, and you certainly don't want to encounter break-ups in your domestic environment unless you can possibly help it. This is why it is imperative for you to deal with any problems in a realistic way. It could make the situation a great deal easier and avoid any unnecessary upheavals which might have a devastating effect on your rather conservative character.

However, if you have realized that it is possible to balance all the areas of your life without neglecting anyone close to you, you may also have discovered that the relationship between you and your partner is mellowing happily into something which may not be the most passionate of involvements, but certainly gives you the companionship and understanding you need.

If your own children are growing up fast, try not to be too strict with them, and don't allow your own criteria to dictate your views on the friends they should have. It is of course necessary to advise them about bad company, drugs and alcohol, but this can be done in a positive way without sounding as if you are preaching.

This is often the time when you begin to enjoy home comforts more and more. But your health will still depend a great deal on the way you look after your mind and body.

You may have assistants and secretaries surrounding you now in your working life. You are unlikely to have changed jobs many times, as it gives you a greater feeling of achievement to climb steadily up from the bottom of a company where perhaps you started as a teenager many years ago.

If you have not needed to work, you might decide to look around for something now that your family is growing up and you have lots of free time on your hands. Your administrative abilities could probably be put to good use helping out on your local council, involving yourself with charities, or with Social Service work.

Capricorn, by now you should have realized that having Saturn, the old taskmaster of the Zodiac, as your planetary ruler, has instilled in you a great deal more patience and self-discipline than the rest of the signs. If at times you were depressed and unduly pessimistic, it is too late to undo the past. However, Saturn's influence is constructive, and can bring you a great deal of wisdom and tranquillity if you are prepared to approach the rest of your life even more positively, and that should also mean that you no longer insist on taking a ringside seat when other people are enjoying themselves, but that you sometimes join in the fun too.

35–45 *and onwards*

AQUARIUS

The years go by, but a typical Aquarian will almost always be idealistic and youthful. However, as you are supposed to be the sign of tolerance, human brotherhood and to have a sense of responsibility towards the world, surely you should have learnt by now that loved ones will only accept your casual approach to them for a limited period of time, especially if your intellectual responses seem to lack the humanitarian feelings you preach.

Stop being so concerned about the future that you forget the present. You may well feel happier when space travel is an everyday occurrence, but that day has not arrived yet, and whilst way out views are often considered natural amongst young people, once you begin to approach middle age it becomes ridiculous. Just because you are considered a Fixed sign, it doesn't mean that *all* your opinions have to be so fixed as well. You keep expecting partners and colleagues to accept your changes of mood even when you know you are being perverse, so how can you expect to be loved and admired? At this stage of your life your mind should be more disciplined.

Physical love is often less important to your sign than mental communication, and if you and your partner are drifting apart, it is imperative that you accept this and decide whether you are genuinely happy with the situation or not. A person who continually discusses reforming the world without seeing the cracks in his or her own environment should be made aware of this inconsistency.

Many Aquarians manage to enjoy a perfect marriage, so unless your own horoscope appears to be an astrological battlefield there is no reason why you should not be able to improve your relationships.

Your children will probably have realized by now that you cannot always be considered a conventional parent. If however your inability to express physical affection has led to your being misunderstood in the past, make sure that your children know that you really love them.

Hopefully, your home can cater for entertaining, or for holding weekly meetings for your favourite charity committee. You will never lose your love for company. It helps to keep your mind alert, and gives you the opportunity to discuss your many ideas with a variety of people.

You should have learned to cope with your health problems, but if you become irrationally touchy when you don't get a good eight hours' sleep, make sure you don't over-tire yourself.

Don't be frightened that with the passing of the years someone younger might take your place at work. Your instinct will always enable you to be one stroke ahead of the rest of us, and if problems do arise you are invariably able to solve them successfully. However, if you have been working your way up to the top of your chosen field, just remember that it can sometimes be a little unnerving for your employees to never quite know what mood you may be in from one day to the next. You are better working amongst other people, and you should not discipline yourself to a one man or one woman occupation unless you really know it is right for you personally.

Aquarians tend to spend money recklessly, so if this is one of your faults do make sure you have a friendly bank manager or accountant who can help you with professional advice, so that your savings don't start to dwindle away at a time when you may desire more comforts in your life.

Aquarius, you so often go through life attempting to change the world, and sometimes you may be successful, but you should have realized by now how necessary it is to relate to the rest of us just a little more.

Don't be a slave to routine, but use your intuition to understand the needs of the people you love and who love you and you will be making a more positive success of your sign.

35–45 *and onwards*

PISCES

In a world where people are continually rushing about with hardly a thought for anyone other than themselves and their own immediate families, it is refreshing to meet Pisceans who are not only aware of other people's suffering, but do genuinely try to do something to relieve it.

However, your own life can often do with a little extra help especially at this stage. The truly positive Piscean should have risen above feelings of insecurity and self-doubt by now, but perhaps there are many of you who are prone to self-pity and discontentment with lives which have failed to live up to earlier expectations.

This certainly doesn't mean you should fear the future, or start to escape more and more into your flights of fantasy when the outside world seems to offer you little hope for happiness just because you have reached the thirty-five plus stage. Stop exaggerating and thinking of yourself as worse off emotionally and materially than anyone else. I know one Piscean who constantly talks to his partner about feeling less privileged than the rest of their friends, and yet this same Piscean has a creative talent which if he did but realize it is envied by a great many of the people that he himself is envying.

You have passed the first Saturn return and probably ironed out the rough patches in your life, but difficulties do not always arrive at the same time. Perhaps you are now beginning to realize that the marriage or relationship which has been drifting on has suddenly reached a point of no return, and the walls of your existence are tumbling down around you. However, surely you have learnt enough to know by now that your philosophy and inner strength comes to the fore when there are real problems to face. Just because you are known for being submissive, this doesn't mean you don't have a duty to yourself.

By now you should be aware of what romance means for you, that it isn't only moonlit walks along country lanes, but can also be found in books, music and films. If physical romance has gone out of your marriage but tender companionship and understanding have remained it is certainly not on the rocks, but may be more stable than before. It is important for you now to clarify your own inner needs, and avoid being up in the clouds about matters which need a practical approach.

If you use your sensitivity and intuition constructively, you certainly shouldn't have to complain about your emotional life from now on.

This can be a wonderful time for you if marriage has reached the stage where you feel completely in tune with your partner, and when your children are giving you a great deal of pleasure as you watch them grow up. Your sympathy and understanding over childhood and adolescent problems cannot be criticized but you sometimes have a habit of playing on the affections of your children and becoming an overly possessive parent. Make sure you don't continually treat them as babies and try not to cling to them as they are growing up. John Ruskin wrote "Give a little love to a child, and you get a great deal back", and true as this may be, it certainly shouldn't be demanded or expected.

Your life-style will if anything become even more relaxed and easy going as you grow older, although the exception proves to be true sometimes as I know one Piscean who already into her fifties plays tennis against seventeen-year-olds as if she was a teenager herself. It is impossible to lay down a hard and fast rule when generalizing about a Sun sign, but you should certainly know your own bodily requirements even more by now. It may be necessary to remind you again, however, of the Pisces tendency to find the lure of alcohol irresistible.

Pisces, you sometimes are a martyr, sacrificing yourself for husband, wife, children, parents, many years of your life, and as long as you are aware of this all is well. It is pointless, however, to turn round at forty or forty-five and say that you have wasted a great deal of your life helping other people, because generally it was your choice. If, therefore, you are feeling sorry for yourself, then resolve to be a great deal more positive from now on, because there is still time ahead of you to enjoy yourself.

Your creative qualities may have lain dormant, and suddenly as you start to remember some of your childhood dreams you may discover a talent for writing. You may have settled into a working life which, because it is helping you towards the financial stability so vital for your existence, is making you forget some of your original aims. Don't allow yourself to become lazy, Pisces, because if you do have special qualifications they should be developed. If your family is growing up, you may even discover that in the future you can turn a hobby such as painting or pottery into a useful and productive side-line.

Pisces, the way you organize your life often stems from your instinct and you turn your back on realism. No one can deny that you genuinely want to be of service to the world, but it is about time that you realized you owe yourself a little more understanding, considering the way you are prepared to put yourself in other people's places so much of the time.

If you resolve to be more realistic and practical from now on, you really will be a positive Piscean, and still have some quiet moments for dreaming too.

SUMMARY

Having read about your Sun sign, and the signs of the people closest to you, hopefully you will have managed to gain some extra insight into personalities and characteristics, which will, in turn, have enabled you to lead a more positive life.

You will also have learnt that "being positive" can sometimes mean toning down some of your own basic characteristics in order to make other people happier, for the definitions of "positive" can also include being opinionated, dictatorial and dogmatic.

Having spent the very last week of this writing commitment sitting with my typewriter on the terrace of an enchanting little house high above the sea, with a magnificent view in front of me, and an air of tranquillity all around, I must also honestly admit that being positive can be helped a great deal by one's surroundings.

In today's world, it is sometimes extremely difficult to find the necessary moments of peace and quiet in which to calm our busy minds.

However, this has only served to make me more convinced than ever that learning to understand yourself and your behaviour in a way which enables you to extricate yourself from difficulties and re-organize your life in a more constructive way is vital.

Maybe you always will be a critical Virgo who notices a mark on the table cloth when you enter a restaurant, or a Piscean who invariably ends the week with a deficit in the household accounts, but you still have time to enjoy the rest of your life being just a little wiser.

SATURN
through the signs

ARIES	March 20th 1908–May 16th 1910
	April 25th 1937–March 19th 1940
	March 4th 1967–April 29th 1969
	April 7th 1996–February 28th 1999
TAURUS	May 17th 1910–July 6th 1912
	March 20th 1940–May 8th 1942
	April 30th 1969–June 18th 1971
	March 1st 1999–2001
GEMINI	July 7th 1912–August 24th 1914
	May 9th 1942–June 19th 1944
	June 19th 1971–August 1st 1973
CANCER	August 25th 1914–October 17th 1916
	June 20th 1944–August 2nd 1946
	August 2nd 1973–September 16th 1975
LEO	October 18th 1916–August 12th 1919
	August 3rd 1946–September 18th 1948
	September 17th 1975–July 25th 1978
VIRGO	August 13th 1919–October 7th 1921
	September 19th 1948–November 20th 1950
	July 26th 1978–September 20th 1980

LIBRA	October 8th 1921–September 13th 1924
	November 21st 1950–October 22nd 1953
	September 21st 1980–November 28th 1982
SCORPIO	September 14th 1924–December 2nd 1926
	October 23rd 1953–October 10th 1956
	November 29th 1982–November 16th 1985
SAGITTARIUS	December 3rd 1926–March 15th 1929
	October 11th 1956–January 5th 1959
	December 17th 1985–February 13th 1988
CAPRICORN	January 21st 1900–January 19th 1903
	March 16th 1929–February 23rd 1932
	January 6th 1959–January 3rd 1962
	February 14th 1988–February 6th 1991
AQUARIUS	January 20th 1903–April 12th 1905
	February 24th 1932–February 14th 1935
	January 4th 1962–March 23rd 1964
	February 7th 1991–January 28th 1994
PISCES	April 13th 1905–March 19th 1908
	February 15th 1935–April 24th 1937
	March 24th 1964–March 3rd 1967
	January 29th 1994–April 6th 1996

These are the overall dates for the years, but Saturn can sometimes retrace its steps into the preceding sign during its passage, and an Astrological Ephemeris for the year of your birth will confirm the exact position of Saturn in your birthchart.